GHOST TOWNS OF
ONTARIO
VOLUME 1 · SOUTHERN ONTARIO

RON BROWN

STAGECOACH

STAGECOACH PUBLISHING CO. LTD.
P.O. Box 3399, Langley, B.C. V3A 4R7

Typesetting, layout and design by
Mainland Graphics Ltd.

Printed in Canada by
D.W. Friesen & Sons Ltd.

First Printing — April 1978
Second Printing—January 1979

Canadian Cataloguing in Publication Data

Brown, Ron, 1945-
    Ghost towns of Ontario

    Includes bibliographies and indexes.
    Contents: v. 1. Southern Ontario.
    ISBN 0-88983-018-5
    ISBN 0-88983-020-7 pa.

    1. Cities and towns, Ruined, extinct, etc. -
Ontario. 2. Ontario - History. I. Title.
FC3072.B76   971.3'03   C78-002050-2
F1058.B76

CONTENTS

ROADS OF BROKEN DREAMS

'ROUND THE BAY

MINING TOWNS OF
SOUTHERN ONTARIO

INTRODUCTION

"Anybody want to see a ghost town?" asked a member of our church youth group from his perch on a rock overlooking Parry Sound's blue waters. With a sunny summer afternoon to kill, the group responded with enthusiasm. That in 1964 was my introduction to the fact of ghost towns in southern Ontario. Up until then, I, like most Ontarians, had given them little thought in the assurance that the nearest ghost town lurked nowhere nearer than the Arizona desert.

That jaunt to the scattered foundations and hulking ruins of what was once Ontario's most promising natural deep water harbour—Depot Harbour—embedded in me an undying enthusiasm for the relics of Ontario's vanished past.

From that day I began compiling a list of ghost towns, scribbling down the name whenever I read it or heard of it. Occasionally, during the course of a leisurely drive in the country, I would 'come across' a ghost town. Then in 1974 the course of my job permitted me to review the history section of our departmental library. There in the local histories of townships and counties I encountered frequent references to ghost towns. The list rapidly grew longer. During lunch hours spent in Ontario's Archives, pouring over microfilms and digging through dusty old documents, I compiled comprehensive historical profiles for each ghost town on my list.

Then came the field work. Following air photo interpretation I turned my car towards Ontario's old ports and millstreams, her remote byways and even isolated islands to record the remnants and to talk with any old-timers with memories of days gone by. At that time the possibility of a book was furthest from my mind. However, friends and colleagues, sharing my enthusiasm for Ontario's ghost towns, planted the seeds of publication and this book gradually began to take form.

History, they say, is dull. I don't believe it. Although history can be *made* dull, it is in fact exciting and meaningful. By writing southern Ontario's history in terms of its ghost towns, I am trying to bring to light one of the many interesting facets of her past, one which has been to date ignored. By doing so, I hope to lure Ontarians away, for even just a few hours, from the more popular, yet foreign dominated, forms of media and make them more aware of their own fascinating heritage. If I am even partly successful in this, I consider my efforts amply rewarded.

Thus I present "The Ghost Towns of Southern Ontario". I hope the reader has the same fun following his arm-chair excursions to the ruins of these ghost towns as I had on their actual trail.

Ron Brown, Toronto
August 5, 1977

ACKNOWLEDGEMENT

Many people have earned my gratitude for their assistance in the production of this work. Most contributed specific information and are acknowledged at the end of the book. There are, however, many friends and relatives who fed me and bedded me on my many field excursions, who gave of their weekends to provide company on my seemingly endless jaunts to weedy fields and ramshackle ruins, and who provided encouragement when energy and interest began to fail.

But supreme acknowledgement belongs to one person—my wife, June—who endured long and tiring ghost town trips in weather fair and foul and who spent over her typewriter too many hours to count producing literally thousands of sheets of draft manuscript. It is to her I dedicate this book.

1

THE RISE AND FALL OF ONTARIO'S VILLAGES

"Ghost towns in Ontario? *Southern* Ontario?" Skepticism marked the first of many questions which greeted my intention to write of ghost towns in southern Ontario. "Surely ghost towns occur only in the United States' deserts or British Columbia's gold fields, but not in such an affluent and growing area as this!" Toss aside such misconception for southern Ontario abounds in ghost towns. A long and varied history has left a legacy of abandoned settlements far more colourful than that of more famous ghost town regions. Here lie the stories of military towns, the old wharves of port towns, and the remote remains of fishing islands, as well as lumber towns, mining towns, milling towns and the short-lived colonization road towns.

Most modern Ontarians are guilty of viewing their history through the single dimension of 1977, barely acknowledging a pioneer phase somewhere "way back when". Ontario however has passed through many colourful phases; each phase fostered villages tailored to meet the needs of the day. As times changed, so changed the villages—changed or died. For if the villages which sprang up during one phase could not change to accommodate the requirements of subsequent developments, they passed out of existence. Ontario's phases were, simply: the military, the pioneer, the agricultural, the expansion, the urbanization and the "land-grab."

The earliest stage of development to bring permanent settlement to the wilds of Ontario was the *military* phase. Through the 18th century and the first two decades of the 19th century colonial defense was paramount. The plan of then Governor John Graves Simcoe was to establish amid the wilderness of southern Ontario a system of "bridgeheads" linked by military roads, each bridgehead to consist of a military garrison, a village to supply skilled trades and craftsmen, and an agricultural community to supply food.

Several bridgeheads subsequently developed into sizeable towns,

due primarily to the growing use of the old military highways. Often however the smaller "bridgeheads" were planned and located only to meet military ends with little thought to future industrial or business needs. Once the military phase passed, those bridgeheads which failed to attract new industries lost their reason for existing and became Ontario's first ghost towns.

With the close of the American Revolutionary War in 1783, waves of Loyalist refugees streamed northward across the border and launched Ontario's *pioneer* phase. The American Revolution was a war supported by only one-third of that population. A third were neutral while the remaining one-third opposed the war and remained loyal to England. The latter were regarded with suspicion by those favouring the war and became the targets for persecution, property damage and personal attacks. To ease the plight of the Loyalists, the British government offered assisted settlement in the Canadian colonies. Between 1783 and 1797 tens of thousands of "United Empire Loyalists" streamed northward, many to Ontario. After 1800 this flow slowed to a trickle. With the dawn of the new century settlers began arriving from Europe and the British Isles, some enticed by various colonization schemes, others driven from their homeland by low wages, oppressive landlords and over-crowding.

Bustling new mill villages on Ontario's rushing mill-streams characterized the pioneer phase. Roads during this period were rudimentary at best but more usually non-existent. Pioneer mills vital to the fledgling farms were few and far between. The farmers often had to walk many miles and then wait for a few days. General stores, shops and taverns were thus essential businesses in the milling communities. Stores and shops provided supplies, blacksmiths, shoemakers and other tradesmen tended to the variety of needs which arose on Ontario's remote pioneer farms, while hotels and taverns eased the waiting and offered rare opportunities to socialize. Some sites had sufficient water supply to entice other pioneer industries such as distilleries.

Slowly, steadily, the hard-working farmers cut down the forests, cleared the stumps, replaced their log shanties with frame or stone houses and established a prosperous agricultural economy. By 1850 much of the pioneer phase had passed and the *agricultural* phase was well underway.

During this stage road networks improved markedly and farmers' businesses moved to road locations which were more accessible than the old mill sites. In instances where main roads passed through existing mill villages, those villages grew; where the roads bypassed them, they shrank, often leaving only the mill. The agricultural phase witnessed the denuding of the forests with devastating results for the

---

Ontario's development is illustrated in these three photos: the top showing the crude initial clearing, log shanty and isolation of the pioneer phase. The center illustrates the agricultural phase when negotiable roads were finally built, when better log homes replaced the original shanty and crops appeared. The bottom illustration represents the expansion phase when businesses blossomed along improved roads, when fine homes and substantial barns were built, when mills hummed, and no more land remained to be cleared.

old mills. Not only was the timber supply soon gone but the sudden absence of the forest cover which had controlled water flow in the streams created raging spring floods and low summer flow. Then, with the invention of the steam mill, which required no water power, the original mill sites lost their attractions and many villages which depended exclusively upon water power vanished.

If the agricultural phase caused the disappearance of many old mill villages, it caused the development and growth of many others. Country needs were many and, due to bad roads and slow transportation, had to be close at hand. Old mill villages situated on the new roads grew into busy country villages while crossroads locations came alive with shops and small industries. A typical country village usually included a gristmill (if on a power site), a carriage works, woollen mill, cheese factory (in the latter years of the 19th century), sawmill (provided there remained a supply of timber), pail factory, or lime kiln; such retail businesses as a general store, or a hotel (if on a major road); such institutions as a church, Orange Hall, or town hall, and any of a number of tradesmen such as blacksmiths, coopers, carpenters, tailors, shoemakers, dressmakers, saddlers or harnessmakers. Many country villages also boasted doctors and veterinarians.

Then came the *expansion* phase and with it the opening of new lands and the growth of new frontier villages. By 1850 southern Ontario's available farmlands were occupied, yet the demand for new land failed to subside. Land-hungry immigrants streamed in, and established farmers sought more land for their sons. Faced with this population crisis, the government acquired and opened to settlers two hitherto unsettled areas: the Queen's Bush and the Ottawa-Huron Tract. The Queen's Bush, defined today by the counties of Grey and Bruce and adjacent portions of Huron, Wellington and Dufferin, was, until then, Indian territory. The Ottawa-Huron Tract covered a vast forested rockland between Georgian Bay and the Ottawa River. Eager settlers flocked in and many villages sprang up at mill sites or at strategic stopping places along the settlement roads. However hope turned to despair as large portions of the new areas were found to possess expanses of bare rock, stony, infertile soils and short growing seasons. Then, like a saving grace, the fertile soils of the Canadian West were thrown open to settlement. The exodus was swift—greater than any southern Ontario had ever known. Many mill villages and stopping places throughout both the Queen's Bush and the Ottawa-Huron Tract died after only a short lifespan.

Expansion also led to the growth of many fishing, lumbering and shipping villages around Georgian Bay. The rapid growth of southern Ontario's cities and those in neighbouring American states led to a marked increase in demand for food and lumber. New railway lines to Georgian Bay markedly improved the access to its resources. But so sudden and so intensive was exploitation that the resources were soon exhausted and the fishing and lumbering villages died.

As Ontario's pioneer fringe swept forward, prospectors and miners probed the ground for mineral wealth. That vast pre-Cambrian mountain root, the Canadian Shield, possessed a great variety of minerals. In its valleys sprang up many dusty, noisy mining villages

10

which thrived for the few years that the small mineral deposits bore fruit, then faded away.

Railway building peaked during this phase. Eager to tap timber, farm produce, and minerals, railway sponsors pushed a dense network of railway lines over Ontario's farmlands and through her forests. At sidings and at stations which existed solely for the preparation and export of various products many small villages popped up and prospered until resources were depleted.

Throughout the second half of the 19th century rural Ontario abounded with country villages that were nearly identical. Then, as Ontario entered its *urbanization* phase, the era of the country village began to close. Seldom did the towns "bust;" rather their demise was gradual, industry by industry. Gristmills were defeated by the decline in wheat farming which, once Ontario's farming mainstay, fell victim in the 1860s and 70s to foreign tariffs and to the killer "midge" disease. When the success of the temperance movement ended liquor sales, many hotels closed their doors for good.

Railways which sprawled across the province between 1853 and 1900 gave insurmountable advantages to towns and villages along their rights-of-way and backwater villages watched many trades and businesses move away to railside. Scales of economy also began to change. Big was better and the one-man shops, the wagon-makers, the harnessmakers, the cobblers and tailors became a thing of the past. General stores and blacksmiths were the last holdouts. However, with the introduction of rural mail delivery in the years prior to the First World War, farmers no longer had to travel to the store to collect mail and the loss of this business closed many a store. Then, in the 1920s and '30s, when the tractor and automobile replaced the horse, most blacksmiths set aside their bellows for the last time.

The urbanization years brought a spate of highway building and road paving. Enjoying sudden access to larger towns, rural residents by-passed many of the old country villages where they formerly did all their shopping. Competition from highway transportation closed many of the smaller rail lines and villages which depended upon this link faded.

Mechanized farming meant larger farming operations and many small farms were bought up by more prosperous farmers. The residual population moved to the rapidly growing cities in search of work so that, throughout most of the present century, rural Ontario has witnessed a long and steady process of depopulation.

In the 1950s and '60s the flight from the countryside suddenly reversed itself and the *"land grab"* phase commenced as the crush of city life sent many city dwellers searching for more peaceful rural surroundings. Vastly improved transportation facilities widened city commutersheds and the pastoral countryside fell within the urbanites' grasp. To the quiet farmlands came two breeds: the wealthy urbanite seeking the status of a "country home," and the idealistic "back-to-the-land" proponent who rejected urban society to identify with "rural roots". The vacant lots in, and the farmlands around several old ghost towns held out both practical and aesthetic appeal and thus, today, a number of ghost towns are, in part, springing back to life.

Convinced now that Ontario's history did in fact produce a rich variety of ghost towns, aspiring "ghost towners," waxing more curious, would ask, "Well, where are they—they must all lie in remote areas." Another misconception.

Southern Ontario's ghost towns are ubiquitous. They are everywhere from the Quebec border on the east to the American border on the west and between the Lower Great Lakes on the south and the French River on the north. To organize this distribution, each chapter concentrates upon distinctive regions within southern Ontario and reflects the stages of Ontario's history which caused the rise and fall of those villages. Each region in turn is divided into smaller "sub-regions" to reflect local geographic characteristics or events.

For example, "*St. Lawrence Lowland*", in eastern Ontario comprises Chapter Two. It was settled during the early pioneer days by United Empire Loyalists and is a large and low-lying plain with three distinct sub-regions; the rocky hills of Leeds county with the ghosts of pioneer mill villages; the limestone plain bordering the Rideau River with its Canal villages; and a sub-region of fertile soils north of the Rideau with its crossroads villages.

The "*Lake Ontario Shoreline*", Chapter Three, encompasses not only the entire Lake Ontario Shoreline but also a large hinterland. "The Loyalist Strand" region reflects village growth during the Loyalist period; early pioneer mill towns characterize the "Gulches and Hollows" between Trenton and Toronto, while the varied villages "Over the Divide" grew up following the conquest of the hilly Oak Ridges barrier. By contrast, the growth of villages "Twixt Lakes Erie and Ontario" in the Niagara Peninsula occurred at different times and for various reasons. Those unlikely ghost towns "In the Shadow of the City" were thriving long before the city, Toronto, was casting a shadow of more than a handful of wooden buildings.

As settlement later moved westward onto the fertile lands of *Ontario's Western Plains,* milling and industrial villages sprang up, from the factory towns of the now defunct Grand River Canal on the "Lower Grand Valley" to the quiet farming villages of the "Upper Grand Valley." Early pioneer mill villages and an old fort appear on the "Old Erie" shoreline, while the "Roads to London" describes the ghosts of farming and milling villages in that area. "Southwestern Ontario" contains an interesting cluster of ghost towns.

"*The Queens Bush,*" or the modern Grey-Bruce region, was purchased as a block to relieve the population pressures on the southern fertile plains. Its sub-regions "The Huron Slopes," "The Uplands" and the "Valley of the Pine" are geographical rather than historical, while the "Willow Creek Controversy" probes a ghost town lost in the annals of time and surrounded now by debate over its very existence.

"*Roads of Broken Dreams*" tells of that futile effort to lure land hungry settlers to that network of difficult bush trails (grandly misnamed colonization "roads") in the barren rocky wilds of the Ottawa-Huron Tract. Several roads have their own stories of hardship and vanished villages: "The Muskoka Road," "The Hastings Road," "The Opeongo Road," "The Addington Road," "The Nipissing Road" and the "Booth Line Railroad." (The latter, obviously, is not a colonization road proper but exhibited similar characteristics.)

Although the villages "*Round the Bay*"—Georgian Bay—developed at different times and for different reasons as reflected in the subchapters "Lumbering Days," "Fishing Islands" and "Days of Steam," all looked to the waters of the Bay for their economic lifeblood.

Southern Ontario's mineral riches occurred in such abundance in Eastern Ontario that the abandoned *Mining Towns of Eastern Ontario* require an entire chapter. Although abundant, the mineral deposits had one common fatal flaw—they were all small and this led to the eventual demise of the towns they supported. Each sub-chapter is devoted to the tale of each mineral—gold, iron, graphite, lead and corundum—and the towns they created—and destroyed.

Now that the ghost town enthusiast has guided himself through the chapters of Ontario's history and across her ghost town regions the next question invariably is, "How did you find out about so many of them?" Sources abound. Fortunately, Ontarians often take particular interest in the history of their locality and library shelves are crammed with books on township histories, county histories and village histories. More often than not, a "local" ghost town is enough of a novelty to warrant a few paragraphs. Newspaper travel columns have on occasion described tours to ghost towns. Modern accounts, however, do not blanket the whole of southern Ontario. Dusty old documents have yielded a storehouse of ghost towns. Around 1860, and between 1875 and 1900, the county atlas became popular. Most showed all existing villages, complete with buildings, owners and businesses. As this period represented the peak of country village development, these atlases provide a rare contemporary glimpse of their palmy days. A comparison of the villages of then with those of today pinpoints ghost towns remarkably well.

Unfortunately the quality of these atlases tends to vary. A second corroborating source was necessary and that was the business directory. Around 1850 business directories began appearing in Ontario. They listed each village, the businesses in them, and often a geographic description. Local residents have also been a valuable treasure-house of information. Stories passed from generation to generation—or even first-hand recollections—have reconstructed many a ghost town. During the course of an interview or exchange of correspondence, local residents have often pointed to other such towns in the vicinity. A final source has been the ghost towner's instinct. When driving through the country, or when scanning maps or aerial photographs, the seasoned ghost towner can recognize those tell-tale characteristics which spell out "ghost town:" an old mill site, a fading pattern of streets, or weedy yards. It is, however, bad research to rely upon one source alone to verify a ghost town and corroboration of two or more of the above sources is imperative.

Many were curious as to "what constitutes a ghost town?" This question has no hard and fast answer. What is a ghost town to some historians fails to make the grade for others. My own definition is "a town that is a mere ghost of what it was." Any village that engenders a feeling of former grandeur, or inspires a sense of abandonment, has been worth investigating. Generally its peak population should have been more than 100 for, at that point, the locality became more than just a small random cluster of rural residences and became an urban entity. It also should have had a number of business functions. A mere one or two functions did not a village make, for literally thousands of Ontario's crossroads possessed a general store and a church or blacksmith shop which exist no more. For a ghost town, total abandonment is preferable but not essential. Even the "classical" ghost towns of the southwestern United States and the interior of British Columbia contain a "resident hermit" or a handful of families. However, if a business continues to function, then no matter how great its original size, the village can have scant claim to ghost town status for it is still perpetuating a village function.

A few skeptics have shrugged, "So who cares?" Others have more delicately worded the question: "What remains at your ghost towns and to whom are they of interest?" Frankly, that varies. Some towns may excite the relic collector, the old bottle collector; others may interest the photographer or sketcher; the rock collector may spend many an hour among the abandoned mining towns; the nostalgia buff may enjoy the mere sense of history among foundations that were once a thriving village; the more academically inclined historical geographer may find interest in the geographical patterns and historical causes of Ontario's ghost town phenomenon; while the Sunday driver may put them on his list of tours.

The age of the towns often determines the nature of the vestiges. Usually, of the very oldest towns, those that were abandoned prior to 1850, nothing remains—even foundations are a rarity. On the other hand, those abandoned since the First World War often contain striking remnants of their days of glory—overgrown roads, crumbling sidewalks, foundations or vacant buildings. Most ghost towns in southern Ontario were abandoned between the turn of the century and the First World War. Foundations may now be overgrown and some original lots may even sport a new house. Although frame dwellings seldom survived long neglect, stone or brick structures fared better. Old places of business, particularly hotels and general stores, may yet exist and be partially used as private residences. Blacksmith shops or wagon factories are often used for storage. Except for stone mills or mine buildings, industrial structures seldom survived. As most relied on water power, their valley location doomed them for the frequent floods of the later 19th and early 20th centuries washed away most structures in their paths. Institutional buildings, schools, churches, town halls, Orange Halls have come to assume a variety of relic forms—residences, storage or total disuse.

The location too influenced what remains. Old buildings close to urban centres have often been salvaged for their lumber and, occasionally, an old lot built on anew; road widenings may have obliterated the vestiges of those buildings which hugged the sides of the narrow pioneer roads.

Not surprisingly, the farther a ghost town lies from growing cities, the truer are its remains. Vacant buildings, overgrown by weeds, windowless and sagging, remain unaltered from time of abandonment.

14

Rugged little-used roads add to the isolation and the allure of the remoter village.

Now the skeptic has exhausted his questions and has become an ardent ghost towner. He or she has seen how Ontario passed through many stages of growth and how each stage left behind those villages that could not change with the times. He or she also has general idea where they are, what they are, and what may remain. All he or she need to do now is to journey through the ensuing chapters, to visit Ontario's many ghost towns and learn of their tales of grandeur and their sad demise. ●

2

ST. LAWRENCE LOWLAND

In the shape of a triangle between the St. Lawrence and Ottawa Rivers and Frontenac County, the "St. Lawrence Lowland" is by turn low and level, high and rocky. Where the western portion borders Frontenac County granite hills mingle with pockets of deep soil; amid countless lakes and streams rise the headwaters of the Rideau River. A flat limestone plain with shallow and droughty soils dominates the central portion while the east is characterized by deep fertile plains.

The Revolutionary War in the United States in the 1770s and 80s triggered Ontario's first wide-spread wave of pioneer settlement. During that war and in the decades which followed, American colonists who had remained loyal to England suffered persecution and property loss and fled their American homes fearful for their lives. Ontario then was an untouched wilderness with major military settlements at Kingston, York (Toronto), Niagara and Windsor, and minor garrisons at several other locations. Farming settlements prior to the Loyalist influx were limited to the neighbourhoods of these military garrisons.

16

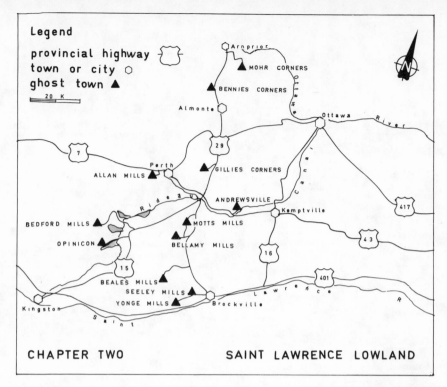

It was in the St. Lawrence Lowland that Ontario's first United Empire Loyalist refugees settled, filling the townships which fronted on the St. Lawrence River.

After the Loyalist influx slowed, the British Isles became the major source of settlers. Scottish Highlanders from the Inverness area, as well as ex-soldiers of the disbanded Scottish regiments, settled much of Glengarry County. Between 1790 and 1820, settlement edged inland from the St. Lawrence along the water highway formed by the Cataraqui Creek, the Rideau Lakes and the Rideau River. Completion of the Rideau Canal in 1832 accelerated the settlement of the Rideau River area and paved the way for the push north of the Rideau between 1830 and 1850.

Most prized were locations with water power. Because of its rivers, the hills of Leeds County were the first to hum with saw and grist mills and give birth to countless mill villages. Farther east, through the counties of Grenville, Stormont and Glengarry, and north through Carlton and eastern Lanark, the terrain is much flatter and millsites fewer. Villages here evolved around stopping places at major road intersections as well as at the few millsites which did exist.

The rise and fall of the Lowland's villages spanned several decades. The earliest to die were the mill villages of Leeds County. When the forest cover disappeared, millstreams dried and the villages died. Even in the more fertile areas villages could not long compete against the combined effects of the railway boom and large-scale urbanization that characterized the closing decades of the 19th century.

A contemporary sketch of the village of Bellamy Mills.

Most of Leeds' towns and villages owe their origins to a rushing water power site on a creek or stream. When millsites were in greater demand than farmland settlers traded away farm lots to acquire a lot with water power.

While many millsites did attract additional businesses and evolve into villages of some size, others faltered and failed. Creeks and streams which had carried a steady supply of water when the land was under forest dried up once the forests were cleared. Where surrounding farms failed to prosper, or where nearby towns drew away the remaining businesses, the mill villages died.

BELLAMY MILLS

Near-impenetrable forests still covered Kitley township in 1798 when Abel Stevens brought the first settlers to the shores of a shallow lake later to become Bellamy's mill pond. On Marshall Creek, which flowed from the lake, John Livingstone found a water power site and there erected a grist mill which served the settlers until 1840 when it was destroyed by fire. To overcome the obstacle of a deep ravine between his mill and the settlers, Livingstone constructed a stone bridge. In 1822 Abraham Kilborn constructed a wooden sawmill at the effluence of the lake, then, in 1840, a short-lived shingle mill near the site of Livingstone's grist mill.

18

Bellamy Mills in busier days during the last century.

In 1855 Chauncey Bellamy arrived and purchased the lot adjacent to Livingstone's and erected a sawmill, a three-storey wooden grist mill, and, downstream, in partnership with Kilborn, a three-storey cheese factory.

Bellamy Mills flourished during the 1860s and '70s. Aside from the mills the village boasted a temperance hall, a Catholic church built in the 1840s, and a daily stage service to nearby Toledo, by then a railway town. While the homes and church stood high and dry on what later became "Bellamy's Hill," the mills nestled in the gully beside.

Then misfortune struck. In 1890 the sawmill which for years had operated day and night closed for repairs and never reopened. Near the end of the century, the church and the cheese factory were moved to other locations. Finally, in 1955, Bellamy's handsome stone mill, long the village's pride and joy, burned. The demise of Bellamy Mills was complete.

Today the ruins of the stone mill tell the story of Bellamy Mills' heyday. Although the cemetery remains, there is no trace of the old church foundations. Old lot lines mark a one-time row of houses overlooking the steep gully. Three original dwellings are still occupied while the old dam holds back the waters of Bellamy Lake as it has done for 130 years.

BEALES MILLS

Ten miles south of Bellamy Mills, near the shores of Charleston Lake, are the little-known remains of Beales Mills. Of Beales Mills' early days little has been recorded beyond the fact that early settlers to these back townships in the 1790s and 1800s recognized the water power potential of a falls on Beales Creek and erected mills on the site.

A mile west, on the north shore of Charleston Lake, the village of Charleston was booming as an important head of navigation. Because Charleston lacked water power the Beales mills were kept busy

19

providing lumber for Charleston's building boom and a steady stream of wagons rattled over the road between the two fledgling villages.

As wheat was king in early Ontario a growing community of pioneer farmers north of Charleston Lake hauled a steady supply of wheat to the grinding stones at the Beales flour mill.

Among Beales Mills' 19th century residents were R. Foxton, N.W. Hawkins, J. Spence (who operated a small store), T. Ross and F. Griffin. The middle 1800s saw the mills on Beales Creek in almost constant production.

But the winds of change which swept Leeds in the late 19th century also swept away Beales Mills. A vastly improved network of roads cost Charleston its role as the head of navigation on Charleston Lake. Then, when wheat farming collapsed, the grist mill fell silent. The final blow fell when the local supply of timber played out and the sawmills closed.

To this day grazing remains the most common form of farming. The road between Charleston and Beales Mills has closed and Beales Creek has dried up. No trace remains of the old mills; even the mill dams are scarcely discernable. Only two of the original buildings still stand. The site is well removed from busy thoroughfares and has remained an undisturbed testimony to an earlier era when mill towns played a vital role in pioneer Ontario.

Only a few buildings remain to mark Motts Mills.

MOTTS MILLS

Eight miles north of Bellamy Mills, a few vacant buildings testify to another of Leeds' once busy mill villages, Motts Mills. In the early 1800s several mills, powered by the waters of Hutton Creek, catered to the needs of the area's pioneers.

In the 1870 and '80s C. Blancher ran the flour mill, G. Blanchard the sawmill, and S. Robinson the shingle mill. The village also boasted a school and a number of private dwellings.

But, like that of Beales Creek, the flow of Hutton Creek became irregular once the forest had been cleared. Because Motts Mills had remained strictly a mill town, when the source of timber for the mills

Old stone inn near the village of Seeley Mills.

became scarce, the mills closed and the settlement died. By 1900 the sounds of industry on Hutton Creek were heard no more.

Today, the old settlement road is a quiet farm land with only five farms along its entire length. Two of the many village buildings have become farm homes and several other outbuildings for the farms. Although the mills have long disappeared, overgrown foundations beside the bridge indicate the location of these early pioneer industries.

SEELEY MILLS

In the southeast corner of Leeds, five miles west of Brockville, grew the village of Seeley Mills. Settlement came early to this corner of Leeds where a dam on Lyn Creek created East Lake and powered the mills. Their operation, however, was short-lived as, by the 1860s, no trace remained of them. In fact, the name had changed to "Selee's Corners," omitting the earlier reference to mills.

About a dozen buildings clustered about Selee's Corners of which J.W. and H. Booth owned most, among them a magnificent stone hotel. W. Niblock operated a spoke factory. At another crossroads a short distance north on property owned by Robert Lee, there existed a small "suburb."

When, after 1880, a branch of the Grank Trunk Railway passed through Selees Corners, the name (and spelling) was changed to Seeley Station.

A few years later, when the branch line closed, the few industries moved and Seeley dwindled. By the 1930s only half of the original buildings remained. By 1976, save the school, nearly all had vanished. Booth's stone hotel is magnificent yet even in its ruin, while, at Lee's corner, all is abandoned, the buildings empty and the yards overgrown.

21

YONGE MILLS

In the 1780s when United Empire Loyalists settled the St. Lawrence shoreline, a water power site on Jones Creek, one mile upstream from the St. Lawrence, proved ideal for mills and had the added advantage of a navigable channel to the St. Lawrence River.

In 1850, with a population of 175, Yonge Mills boasted two hotels, complete with taverns, run by William Armstrong and Thomas Marshall respectively; Bill Baxter's general store, James McElhinney's sawmill, a fulling mill run by F. Jones, and two blacksmith shops. Daily stages bounced along a crude road to Brockville, some 12 miles distant, for a fare of two shillings and six pence. In the 1860s and '70s, James Parr opened a clothing factory and Osmond Jones a flour and sawmill. By 1879 B. Burnham had taken over the general store. The village by this time had added a pair of temperance halls.

Most of the buildings clustered around the original power site. But in the 1860s, after the Grand Trunk Railway opened its main line across the little plain one-half mile north of the original village, a number of buildings popped up around the crossing and, for a time, there were two "Yonge Mills".

Near the end of the 19th century, with the decline in the wheat and timber trades, Yonge Mills' industries suffered a setback from which they never recovered. Even a new cheese factory failed to revive the village and, by 1914, only Burnham's store remained. Although a few residents lived on at Yonge Mills after the war, the shops and industries had closed their doors for good.

Then the automotive age ushered in newer and wider highways. The old Brockville road which once twisted over the ridge and through the gully underwent a major re-alignment, bridging the gully and by-passing the old village. Then, in the 1950s and '60s, increasing highway traffic proved too great for the two-lane roadway and there appeared a new super-highway, the MacDonald Cartier Freeway which skirted the village to the south.

Sandwiched now between the two thoroughfares, the old village site retains few vestiges of its days of glory. Traces of the mill remain but the hotel has long vanished. Of the cheese factory only a chimney looms above the weeds while Burnham's store has become a private residence. Amid the few remaining original residences, both by the millsite and by the railway crossing, foundations and abandoned buildings abound.

ALONG THE RIDEAU:

One of southern Ontario's most historic rivers is the Rideau River. Rising north of Kingston in the picturesque Rideau Lakes, it flows eastward under the shadow of rocky cliffs and meanders through lush farmlands to its cascading confluence with the Ottawa River. Also originating in the Rideau Lakes is a lesser-known stream, the Cataraqui Creek, which flows south to Kingston. Combined, these rivers provided the first "highway" between Kingston and Ottawa and gave settlers access to their inland farmlots between 1790 and 1830.

Although a few small villages had existed at millsites on the Rideau prior to 1832, the opening of the canal in that year greatly accelerated their growth. Where none had previously existed, new villages burst into existence and, by 1840, a string of busy towns and villages dotted the length of the canal as barges shipped their products to market.

The 1850s to 1870s ushered in the railway age and ushered out the canal age. Newer and larger ships which could not fit the shallow draft of the Rideau Canal were confined to the St. Lawrence. Although existing mills and mines continued to ship their products out on the canal, at least until their source materials were depleted, new industries sought railway locations and the canal towns stagnated.

The Rideau Canal has, since the Second World War, experienced another change. As more and more pleasure boaters began to appreciate the beauty of the Rideau Lakes, the historical and architectural treasures of canal villages and the tranquility of the waterway, marinas and tourist shopping facilities have revitalized many sleepy old towns.

In a rare joint planning effort, the federal and provincial governments, through their "Canada-Ontario-Rideau-Trent-Severn" planning exercise (CORTS) are producing plans and policies to preserve the historical and scenic attributes of the waterway. It is hoped that through this exercise the historical heritage of the canal's villages, present and past, will receive the recognition it so richly deserves.

The village of Andrewsville in the years before 1900.

ANDREWSVILLE

Pioneer settler Rufus Andrews provided the initial impetus for this small village on the north bank of the Rideau River in 1843. A mile upstream from the village of Burritts Rapids, he erected a shingle mill and a large dam. Shortly afterward, the government established a post office and named the community after its founder.

The village grew steadily and peaked between 1870 and 1900.

Burrowes' sketches of the Rideau Canal are as unique as they are famous. The Long-Island Waste-weir Dam, shown here under repair, was a short distance downstream from Andrewsville.

Remains of old dam at Andrewsville.

Despite decreasing canal usage, Andrewsville's activities related more closely to the surrounding farming than to river commerce and her fortunes rose and fell with those of the farmers.

By 1870 the village numbered 200 residents and boasted an impressive list of industries and businesses. Benjamin and Thomas Cook operated shingle and grist mills and Henry Watts a sawmill. There were also a carding mill, general store, blacksmiths, sawyers, and labourers and a daily stage service to the riverside towns of Merrickville and Kemptville.

H.R. Beldon, in his 1878 atlas of Lanark County, observed of the village: "Andrewsville at the south-east corner of the township called after Rufus Andrews, the pioneer of the locality which possesses the commercial and artisan facilities usually found in a village of 200 inhabitants including grist, saw, shingle and carding mills and shops of mechanics."

As timber supplies disappeared and as wheat farming changed to dairying, Andrewsville's star began to fade and one by one her industries shut down until, by 1900, only the store, blacksmith shop and sawmill remained. The population had dropped to a mere 50. The village gained only one new industry, W.F. McMahon's cheese box factory, but it had a short life.

Today, Andrewsville has neither industries nor shops; the mill and dams are in ruins. The old streets fade away into bush and most lots are weed-infested. Six original houses have survived the years, some occupied permanently, others only as summer cottages. On a couple of the old Andrewsville lots cottages have recently been constructed. The Rideau Canal lock station still operates and although thousands of pleasure boaters pass through it, few are aware of the ruins behind the riverside bushes that mark the site of the once-busy milling village of Andrewsville.

ALLANS MILLS

Eastern Ontario's mills have a wide reputation for the beauty of their stone-work architecture: the grist mill at Bedford Mills, the Mill of Kintail, the Manotick Mill and, on a tributary of the Rideau River, five miles west of Perth, James Allan's old grist mill.

Although the Perth area was first settled by soldiers of disbanded Highland regiments, there was another source of settlers to the area. In Scotland, the end of the Napoleonic War left a great many craftsmen with little work and sadly decreased wages. With little prospect for improving their lot in Scotland, they asked for and received assistance from the British government in the form of emigration to the Perth and Lanark areas of Upper Canada. The assistance was administered by what were called "Lanark Societies."

Francis Allan was one such "Lanark Society" emigre. After a storm-tossed Atlantic journey on the ship *Atlas* which saw the tragic death of his infant son, Allan arrived in Canada in 1816 and settled on the "Scotch Line," about six miles west of the modern-day village of Perth. Another son, William, born in 1833, eventually acquired a parcel of land, south of the Scotch Line, through which flowed Grants Creek. Using the water power from the creek, William erected a sawmill and a stone grist mill. Across from it he added a store with blacksmith shop attached.

There were many water power opportunities on Grants Creek, and on the Tay River into which Grants Creek flowed, and at most the land-owners erected a grist or sawmill. Thus, within a short distance of Allan's two mills, there were, by 1878, George Oliver's grist mill a few hundred yards downstream, and, north of the Scotch Line, on the Tay River, the Scott brothers' grist and sawmills, McCabe's grist mill, and Wilson's and John Ritchie's sawmills. At the site of William Allan's mills were Pat Fagan, wagonmaker, George Murphy, blacksmith, and Ed Murphy, shoemaker, while Allan himself managed the store and post office. A few shops also appeared at Scott's and Ritchie's mills while a school on the Scotch Line served the entire community. Each mill road led separately to the main roads rather than to the other mills and produced a somewhat scattered village. Stages ran two to three times per week to Perth for 25 cents a fare and to the more distant village of Westport for 75 cents.

The depletion of wheat and timber supplies during the latter years of the 1800s took its toll on Allans Mills. Wide-scale forest clearing closed

(Left) The road past the old stone mill at Allan Mills is used now for scenic driving. (Right) Empty structures stand near one of Allan Mills' many mill sites.

the sawmills, while the change from wheat farming to dairying doomed the grist mills. Allan's grist mill and Ritchie's sawmills were the sole survivors. Watson's and Scott's sawmills and McCabe's grist mill disappeared, Oliver's mill found more practical use as a barn and Scott's grist mill became an electrical power plant named Bowes Mills. Around 1910 the Burgess Milling Company took over Allan's grist mill and operated it until recently.

Ritchie's, now Adam's, old water-powered sawmill, only slightly the worse for wear, still stands, as do several vacant shops nearby. Lumbering on a smaller scale is still carried out at the site. The limestone powerhouse at Bowes Mill, standing amid disused shops, houses interesting artifacts of early electrical power generation. Although Oliver's grist mill looks now like a rather ordinary barn, the residences are magnificent architectural representatives of early Ontario, one a solid stone house, the other a handsome Georgian board-and-batten structure. But Allan's three-storey stone grist mill is the grandest, a fact which, happily, is recognized by its new owners who are restoring and preserving it along with the old general store and adjacent blacksmith shop. William Allan's stone house should not be overlooked. It, too, is one of those stone masterpieces for which the Perth area has developed such a justifiably proud reputation.

BEDFORD MILLS

Forty miles north of Kingston, the power potential of Buttermilk Falls beckoned to a pioneer settler. Benjamin Tett, in 1831, leased from the Crown the site where the waters of Devil Lake cascade down a rocky ridge into Loon Lake on the Rideau Canal. He then sublet it to the Chaffey brothers of Brockville who erected saw and grist mills; the latter at the foot of the cascade, the former at the head. Both were powered by creaking water wheels. The Chaffeys later added a store, boarding house and private dwellings.

Possibly realizing his mistake in subletting such a profitable site, Tett reacquired the property in 1834. One year later, the government

Bedford Mills around 1890, showing saw and grist mills, power house and church.

The original stone Bedford mill is now a fine private residence.

established a post office with the name Bedford Mills, commemorating the Duke of Bedford. Tett's operation was lucrative. As many as 150 men worked the sawmill each spring, preparing great amounts of cordwood, shingles, cedar poles, railway ties and tan bark for shipment by barge down the Rideau Canal.

Over-exploitation of forest resources doomed many an early mill and, by the end of the 19th century, the Tett sawmill operations dwindled to a fraction of their former activity. The Tett brothers, John and Ben Junior, who had taken over their father's holdings, in 1899 turned their attention to the area's rich mica deposits. Mica was popular in those days as a fire-proof transparent shield. The mining and shipping of mica, some sheets as wide as five feet, engaged the remaining residents of Bedford Mills.

Being a non-renewable resource, the mica too played out and in 1908 the mine closed. The ever-enterprising Tett brothers then turned to selling electricity from the new powerhouse at the foot of Buttermilk Falls.

Although they were its biggest, the Tetts were not Bedford Mills' only businessmen. W.H. McBroome operated the stately stone grist mill and in 1890 W.R. Freeman opened a cheese factory.

The village itself developed both on the shore of Loon Lake, a somewhat swampy area, and on a rocky ridge overlooking both Loon and Devil Lakes. In the "lower" town stood the store, the school, St. Stephen's Anglican Church and the grist mill and power house at the foot of the falls. Atop the hill were the boarding house, private dwellings, and nearby the sawmill at the head of Buttermilk Falls. Opposite the mills on Loon Lake, on another ridge, several stately frame homes were constructed. The cheese factory stood a quarter of a mile to the east on a side road. By the 1920s most of the village stood vacant, its residents having sought work in nearby villages; only a few remained in retirement.

A new Perth Road by-pass has left much of this old ghost town intact. Although no traces remain of the cheese factory, foundations mark the school and store and a few of the original dwellings still stand, some now used as summer cottages. The old powerhouse stands dreary and forlorn while, in the rocks of Buttermilk Falls, remain pieces of the old wooden flume. Although silent in the winter, from the stately white frame church, the music of worshippers from nearby summer cottages issues forth each Sunday. The handsome grist mill has become Bedford Mills' beauty mark, and has been remodelled into a fine private residence.

The picturesque remains of this former industrial village have become a recreational side trip for motorists driving on the Perth Road and for boaters cruising the Rideau Canal.

The famous artist Burrowes completed numerous watercolours of the Rideau Waterway during the 1840s. This view dated 1840 illustrates Opinicon Lake when the village of that name was but a fledging nucleation.

The old pioneer schoolhouse at Opinicon.

OPINICON

After the Rideau Canal lost its military role, commercial shipping sparked the rise of many towns along its banks. In the Rideau Lakes area where the land held out meagre prospects for farmers, phosphate deposits and stands of tall timber provided an industrial base for a sprinkling of pioneer villages. At the western end of Lake Opinicon, the most scenic of the Rideau lakes, a small scattered village developed along the rugged rocky shores. Its name: Opinicon.

By 1870 Opinicon contained M. Corkey's hotel, John Poole's sawmill and Darius Warner's store. Nearby farms supplied wheat to Thomas Cook's flour mill and Alex and Cornelius Telpher were among the village's several commercial fishermen.

To add to Opinicon's prosperity, a phosphate mine opened on the shores of a neighbouring lake. A contemporary scribe commented: "The Opinicon mine...is owned by the Canada Company (and) worked in royalty of $2 per gross ton. The work is carried on day and night with two shifts of men, a total force of 30 men being employed... The output... is sorted, washed, and then hauled half a mile to a landing on the Lake (Opinicon) loaded on scows each holding about 100 tons and thence taken to Kingston" (as quoted in an 1893 Ontario Bureau of Mines Report).

A busy canal port, Opinicon in the 1870s and 80s also shipped bargeloads of timber, flour, phosphate and fish down the canal to Kingston for consumption or export.

With the failure of wheat farming in the '80s and '90s, the grist mill closed, although the substitution of dairy farming permitted James Hunter to open a cheese factory and, by the late '80s the village had expanded to include a boarding house, Orange Hall, and school house.

Mrs. Helen Campbell taught at the school house during the early years of this century and has published her recollections. She recalls the days when Opinicon was host to the men toiling on the "People's Railway," and when Auntie Jane, a midwife substitute for the nearest doctor, brought many of Opinicon's babies into the world. But among her fondest memories are those of "Hero," pet dog of Frank and James Dunlop, who faithfully accompanied his young masters across the lake to the school house each morning, then home again each evening.

Most of Opinicon developed on the shores of the lake around what came to be called Telephone Bay. Here stood the mills, cheese factory, store, post office and landing. Along an arduous, twisting dirt road which, eight miles to the west, joined the more travelled Perth-Kingston Road, straggled the school, boarding house, Orange Hall, cooper, church and a few homes.

Soon the timber supply was depleted and the sawmills shut down. When the mill hands left, struggling farmers lost the only market for their produce. The rocky soils, marginal at best, drove most away. The resultant wide-spread depopulation closed the hall, school, church and post office and Opinicon, with no reason to continue, became another Rideau Canal ghost town.

Summer cottagers have brought new life to Lake Opinicon's shores and pleasure boating has replaced the earlier commercial traffic. Sadly, much of the original Opinicon is difficult to find. Although the school house and the "landing" still remain, only traces of the mill and boarding house reward a scrupulous search. The Rideau Hiking Trail crosses the site and the ruins of Opinicon have been a popular destination for hikers into the Rideau Canal's past.

NORTH OF THE RIDEAU:

The area north of the Rideau contained a wide range of farming conditions. Shallow-soiled limestone plains covered a large portion. In several locations the hard pink granite bedrock of the Canadian Shield cropped out through the soil surrounded by extensive areas of level fertile soil.

The earliest settlers were the veterans of the 1812 war, founders of Perth in 1819 and Richmond in 1815. In the 1820s, a crude road linked the two towns. An older road which had linked Kingston with Perth was extended northward from Perth towards the Ottawa River. Along these roads several stopping places and inns were built and around some of them grew small villages. Other villages developed around mill sites.

Throughout the North Rideau area villages remained few in number and small in size. There were several reasons for this: the farming was not uniformly prosperous nor did it enjoy the market accessibility comparable to that in older areas. In the heady days of railway building only two railway lines crossed the area. The growth of Ottawa and other nearby towns gradually lured away the small village businesses. Others closed as they became redundant or obsolete. The villages of North Rideau neither boomed nor busted. The ghost towns met slow rather than sudden deaths.

John Baird built Bennies Corners' "Mill of Kintail" in 1830; it is now the "Tait Memorial Museum".

GILLIES CORNERS

At what was in 1819 a remote curve in the old government road (now County Road 4) between Perth and Richmond, west of present-day Highway 15 north of Smiths Falls, Archibald Gillies opened a licensed hotel. This popular stopping place became known as Gillies Corners. For 20 years Gillies' hotel catered continuously to thirsty and weary travellers before finally closing its doors in the 1850s. Over that time a small village had developed and included a church, a school and a number of private dwellings.

In later years when Ontario's wheat market collapsed and provincial farmers switched to dairying, a cheese factory opened at the Corners but it lasted only a few years. One by one the village's buildings fell vacant. When a major re-alignment of the Perth-Richmond Road by-passed the forlorn ruins, the demise of Gillies Corners was complete.

Time has erased the village and parts of the original Perth-Richmond Road and here the original government road is traceable only on aerial photographs. Where Gillies Corners once flourished, there remain only a few overgrown yards and the now abandoned church.

BENNIES CORNERS

In 1821 James Bennie had acquired a tract of land on the future alignment of the Perth Road extension, about half-way between modern Almonte and Arnprior. With the opening of the road nine years later, in 1830, the intersection at Bennie's lot took on his name and has remained to this day, Bennies Corners.

Although the Corners lacked water power, the rushing Indian River just a hundred yards to the south, possessed ample power sites. There John and William Baird, in 1830, erected a large stone flour mill, a

31

facility much needed by the wheat farmers then filling the area. A few years later Stephen Young constructed a barley mill, a short distance from the Baird mill.

The Snedden family, who had arrived prior to 1821 and acquired several parcels of land, became involved in many of the village's business concerns. James and Alex operated prosperous farms while Dave Snedden opened the Rosebank Hotel just east of the Corners. In later years, William Snedden operated a sawmill.

By the 1860s Bennies Corners boasted a population of 100 and several industries and trades. In addition to the early mills, there were a shoemaker, cooper, tanner, blacksmith, and carpenter. Alex Leishman operated a store and post office while John Allan had constructed the village's second sawmill. Subsequent years saw the construction of a public school where Thomas Caswell taught. William Phillips, blacksmith, expanded his enterprise in the 1860s to include carriage manufacturing.

By the end of the century, the fortunes of Bennies Corners had taken a turn for the worse. The nearby railway village of Almonte was on its way to becoming a busy industrial town. Attracted by the business opportunities in this expanding community, Bennies Corners' businessmen moved from their remote location. Meanwhile the decline in wheat farming and lumbering took their toll on the mills at Bennies Corners. By 1899 the post office had closed and by 1914 Snedden's old sawmill was the sole survivor of Bennies Corners' demise.

Almonte is quieter today but still continues to be the region's main village. However, at Bennies Corners, on the old Perth Road, only the wind blows amid the grasses of the old village lots and around the abandoned schoolhouse.

Baird's Mill of Kintail has since become the Tait McKenzie museum and an attraction to tourists who appreciate its beautiful stonework architecture and the pioneer exhibits on display.

MOHRS CORNERS

For several years after its founding in 1819, the Ottawa River mill town of Fitzroy Harbour had no link with the "Outside" other than via the Ottawa River. After a few years a settlement road was built inland to link with the newly constructed Perth Road extension. It was along this road, in the 1850s, that the son of a German emigrant made his way.

On a gentle hill five miles from Fitzroy Harbour, and only a mile south of modern-day Highway 17, Charles Mohr, son of John C. Mohr, erected a hotel. In those days, when stage travel was painstakingly slow and five to six miles usually a half-day's journey, hotels at these intervals were a welcome relief to weary travellers. Soon other businesses clustered around the hotel and the village of Mohrs Corners was born.

Because of its location on a busy main road, the site was deemed an appropriate location for township administration. The princely sum of 100 pounds for a town hall was granted and a small board and batten building erected.

In 1863 Mohrs Corners was a picture of prosperity. Walling's Atlas showed, at its corners, Mohr's hotel, the town hall, a school and two

Residence of Charles Mohr, Mohrs Corners, ca 1880 (from the Illustrated Historical Atlas of the County of Carlton).

stores operated by Summerville and Hubsch respectively, plus several private dwellings.

But Mohrs Corners was destined to decline shortly thereafter. Only a mile to the north an excellent water power site on the Mississippi River had become the site of a rival village which lured most of the businesses away from Mohrs Corners. For a time it even stole the name. Later it became known as Galetta and Mohrs Corners reassumed its original name but little else. Beldon's account of 1879 reads as follows: "The P.O. was formerly kept at the 'suburb' called Mohrs Corners, a short distance further south, which was until of late the principle (sic) place of the two; but lately all the places of business (including the P.O.) have removed to Galetta."

Today even Galetta and Fitzroy Harbour are no longer the important villages they once were. Indeed, they are now little more than retirement villages. Mohrs Corners is only a relic of its golden days. The red brick school lies empty, all other buildings save two brick houses have disappeared. The town hall met an inglorious fate as a storage shed on a property a mile and a quarter south. Prosperous farms still abound but the once flourishing township capital of Mohrs Corners is little more than a memory. ●

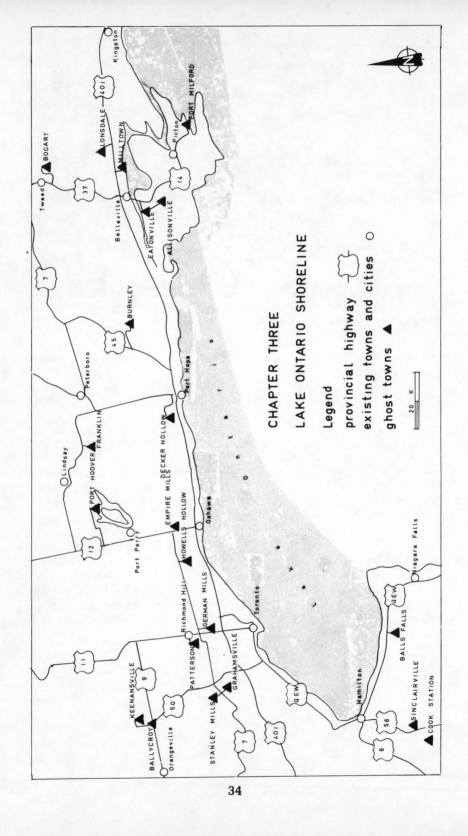

CHAPTER THREE

LAKE ONTARIO SHORELINE

Legend

provincial highway

existing towns and cities ○

ghost towns ▲

20 K

3

LAKE ONTARIO SHORELINE

The "Lake Ontario Shoreline" is Ontario's modern-day heartland. It includes Lake Ontario's shoreline between Kingston and Niagara-on-the-Lake, and hundreds of miles of hinterland defined by lines linking Kingston, Bradford, Georgetown and Port Dover on Lake Erie. Physical conditions within this area vary. The Kingston-Belleville-Prince Edward County section is characterized by an extensive limestone plain with shallow droughty soils. Between Belleville and Toronto, a long ridge of broken sandy hills known as the "Oak Ridges" divides the flat fertile lakeshore plains from the gently rolling terrain to the north.

Entering Upper Canada through Kingston, United Empire Loyalist settlers migrated westward along Lake Ontario's shoreline, across the island county of Prince Edward and on towards Toronto. Water being virtually the only "highway" of the day, the Loyalist farmers tended to settle close to the lakeshore or to navigable rivers.

While the accessible lakeshore plains between Kingston and Toronto were settled between 1790 and 1840, the lands north of the "Oak Ridges" divide saw no concerted settlement until after 1840 when a flurry of road and railway building broached the ridge's few gaps.

Where river mouths and bays afforded harbours of refuge, small port villages sprang up. Where water-powered millsites were either upstream from the harbours or within easy reach, busy mill towns appeared. Where roads and railroads inched inland, villages developed at stopping places, road intersections and river crossings.

Then, with the coincidental shrinking of the forests, the demise of wheat farming, and the trend towards large-scale urbanization near the end of the 19th century, the day of the country village came to a close and many of Lake Ontario's shoreline and inland villages vanished.

35

THE LOYALIST STRAND:

Forty miles west of Kingston lies Ontario's only island county, Prince Edward County. Its level terrain, its many sheltered harbours, and its proximity to the United Empire Loyalist entry point at Kingston made it the earliest and most thoroughly settled county in Ontario. By 1830 the population density reached 25 persons per square mile.

Being on an island, Prince Edward's pioneers relied heavily upon the efficiency of marine transportation. From the middle to late 19th century, no less than a dozen ports were in full swing, building ships and exporting barley to the growing brewing industry in upper New York State. Equally busy were Prince Edward's inland villages located at millsites or at crossroads.

But the little ports and the country villages could not long survive the growing competition from the nearby towns of Belleville and Picton which enjoyed the advantages of deeper harbours, larger ships and railway stations. During the dying years of the 19th and the early years of the 20th century, many of Prince Edward's villages lost their reason for existing. Although many retained some residents and a few shops, the old villages of Eatonville, Allisonville, and Port Milford faded completely.

Of the many rivers and brooks that rush down Ontario's south slope into Lake Ontario, the Salmon River, which enters the Bay of Quinte north of Prince Edward County, enjoyed the best millsites.

By 1850, the Salmon River Valley was alive with a string of mill villages from Shannonville at the river mouth to the appropriately named Milltown, one mile upstream, then Lonsdale, Kingsford, Forest Mills, Roblin and Croydon. In spite of their robust beginnings most dwindled after losing their timber supplies. With the exception of Milltown and Lonsdale, the villages have survived as centres of retirement homes.

ALLISONVILLE

The old winding Wellington-Rednersville stage road is quieter now. Automobile traffic prefers the straighter and wider Highways 14 and 33.

But in the 1830s, half-way along the road, the cascading waters of Consecon Creek powered the early saw and grist mills of Charles and William Allison and gave rise to the village of Allisonville.

In the Picton *Gazette* of 1938 one of Allisonville's residents, Mr. A.L. Calnan, recounted his early days: "My earliest memories of Allisonville are of saw and grist mills...the mills disappeared long ago... Allisonville was quite a fair sized community with several homes and the usual stores and blacksmith shops, etc." Calnan recalled fond memories of watching George Young at his blacksmithing, of the weekly entertainments at the nearby schoolhouses, and of James Boyd, postmaster and manager of the general store.

"James Boyd and his wife came to Allisonville in the early 1880s. Their store was well stocked and for many years was a popular neighbourhood gathering place. In the evening during the summer months the place was crowded." Their store remained in the Boyd family

(Left) Allisonville's cheese factory before 1900.
(Right) Old Orange Lodge at Allisonville is still a handsome structure (1976).

almost until 1960, its last owner being Mrs. Helen Boyd.

George Young, the blacksmith, also ran a tavern during the 1880s, although Young was a teetotaller. There were two asheries where wood ash was manufactured into potash, one operated by one-time store owner, Royal Hicks, the other by Henry Tinklepaugh. Gideon Pine was the village cooper, specializing in barrels and churns. James Robbins and Horatio Titus were other early store owners, while Hiram Forshee, in the '80s, ran a shingle mill. When, in the '80s and '90s, dairying became a popular farming venture, George Ferguson opened a small cheese factory.

As urbanization beckoned industries to larger towns, Allisonville's businesses closed and her residents left. Only the general store survived the exodus and it, too, is now a memory.

In contrast with its peak when Allisonville's population numbered 150, today only two or three families live at the site. The steps which once led to the busy general store are cracked and broken and lead only to an overgrown foundation. Bushes now mark the sites of the cheese factory, the blacksmith shop, the cooperage and all but a couple of homes. The creek runs dry for most of the year and only the outline of the old mill pond remains. The Orange Hall, however, still stands proudly, a handsome example of early Ontario's rural architecture and the lone reminder of a once bustling country village.

EATONVILLE

Farther north along the old stage road stood a much smaller village—Eatonville. Picton's 1937 centennial book, *Picton's 100 Years,* described it: "Ameliasburg (township) has a 'ghost village.' About one and one-half miles east (should read 'south') of Rednersville was once the village of Eatonville. Here stood an old tannery where many a farmer took his cattle hides and got his 'plough boots.' There was a general store...a blacksmith shop...and two or three houses."

Eatonville, however, never achieved proportions greater than a crossroads hamlet and all that remains today are rotting logs, weedy yards and crumbling fencelines.

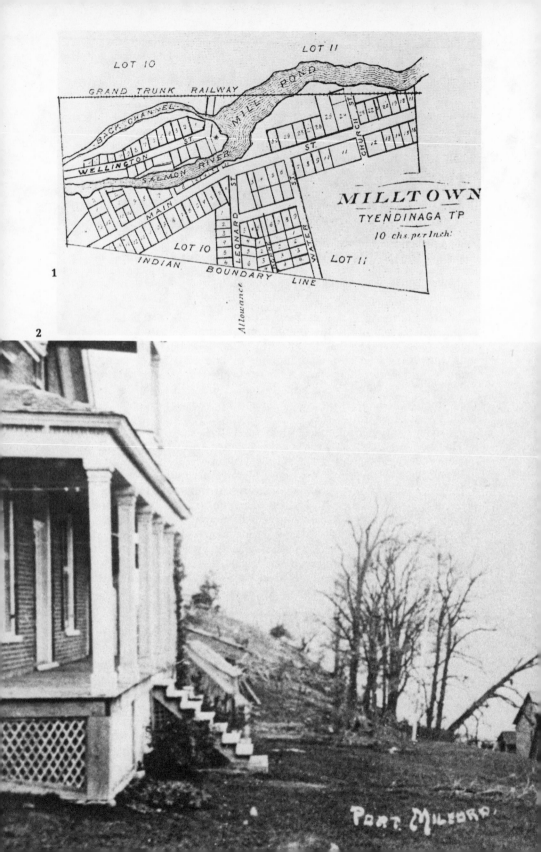

1

2

PORT MILFORD

3

(1) Town plan of the village of Milltown circa 1878. (2) Warehouses and residence at Port Milford probably around the turn of the century. (3) A rare photo of James Cooper sitting at his Port Milford wharf. (4) Port Milford's old general store still retains much original character. (5) The cannery remains cover a large area at Port Milford, 1976.

4

5

PORT MILFORD

The island county of Prince Edward relied almost totally upon water transportation to export produce and to link it with the rest of Upper Canada. Port Milford was just one of more than a dozen ports which ringed Prince Edward's shores. Its location in the sheltered waters of South Bay, a protected harbour on the southeast coast of the island, 10 miles south of Picton, gave it a natural advantage for both shipbuilding and exporting.

Port Milford's birth dates to the arrival from Kingston in the 1860s of a lone hiker with all his possessions in a pack. James Cooper, with his brother, William, proceeded to construct docks, stone warehouses and a general store. When Earl Collier arrived, Cooper built him a fine red brick house which stands to this day. Collier went on to operate the general store after the turn of the century.

A short distance along the shore, A.W. Minaker opened a store, hotel and wharf but, by the 1880s, Cooper owned this as well.

An active ship-building industry developed. George Dixon built the *W.R. Taylor* in 1877, and the McMurchy brothers the *Huron*. Other schooners launched at Cooper's wharf included the *Jennie Lind, Jessie Brown, Marysburg, C.J. Collier, C. Gearing* and *Speadwell*. To guide these ships into the harbour there hung only a lantern on a pole. The remains of the *Fleetwood*, one ship which did not make it, still lie in the offshore waters of the bay.

In its heyday as a port, Port Milford shipped many of Prince Edward's farm products, including butter, cheese, lumber, apples and barley. Although Port Milford's facilities could handle the smaller schooners popular in the mid 1800s, they were not suitable for the larger craft which began plying the lakes toward the end of the century. Picton gradually assumed the role of major, and almost exclusive, port town. Then the coming of the railway in the '80s further focussed growth on Picton.

By 1900, when Port Milford's shipping days ended, the village had turned its attention inward. Since Prince Edward County's farmers had by then become a major producer of vegetables, the Church brothers selected Port Milford as a site for a large cannery. By the 1930s, Canadian Canning Company operated the plant and Port Milford reached a size even greater than in its heyday as a port. Its population edged up to 100, and along its two main streets stood nearly two dozen buildings plus the store, church and school.

In the late 1930s the cannery closed and the glory that was Port Milford slipped into the pages of history. Only a massive stone foundation remains where the cannery stood and of the house-lined road leading to it, only grassy mounds along a dirt track. At the water's edge, Cooper's stone warehouses are reduced to foundations and the wharves to piles of lumber. On the bank above the wharf, Earl Collier's fine brick house still dominates and, opposite it, stands the vacant general store, its name still vaguely visible.

Nearby there is a new and appropriate attraction—a mariners' museum housing a fine display of older marine artifacts and sagas. In a part of Prince Edward County that once looked to the waters of Lake

Ontario, the remains of Port Milford and the mariners' museum are fitting tributes to a bygone way of life.

MILLTOWN

That quiet backwater of Lake Ontario protected by Prince Edward County is known as the Bay of Quinte. Loyalist settlement spilled over from Prince Edward onto the Quinte north shore and spread up the river valleys. The Salmon River Valley, with its considerable water power potential, attracted many settlers who soon opened numerous mills. Around many of these mills little villages formed and, by the 1850s and '60s, the valley was thickly populated. Shannonville, Milltown, Lonsdale, Kingsford, Forest Mills, Roblin and Croydon were the bustling mill towns that dotted the river. Today all the mills are silent and the population sparse.

In the 1830s a waterfall one mile from Shannonville attracted mill owners Lazier and Appleby. Their operations soon attracted a large population and many businesses.

Milltown's village plan, with 10 streets and 112 lots, covered both banks of the river. Main Street, the main road from Shannonville, ran parallel to the river along its east bank and contained no fewer than 21 shops. Wellington and Colborne Streets, along the opposite bank, had five shops. Included among them were three general stores, two carpenters, two wagon makers, a carriage maker, an inn and many small trades.

An 1878 atlas of Hastings County carried this description: "The village of Milltown is appropriately named. This is the third largest village in the township and like the others, is largely engaged in manufacturing. The Messrs. Lazier have a flouring and sawmill which do a large business. N.S. Appleby, M.P.P. and Mr. Burdett carry on the upper mills, manufacturing an excellent brand of flour while the sawmill connected furnishes its quota to the many thousands of feet of

A contemporary sketch of the village of Milltown, 1879 (from the Illustrated Historical Atlas of the Counties of Hastings and Prince Edward)

lumber that are annually shipped from this point. There is also the iron foundry and machine shop of R.F. Pegan (sic) and a cabinet and chair manufactory. Present population about 250," (most being mill hands or foundry workers).

The Appleby grist mill ground as many as 45,000 bushels of flour per year, while the Lazier mill used its three run of stone to churn out 30-40,000 bushels. Both had sawmills attached, the Appleby mill having three saws. Opposite the Lazier mill stood Regan's extensive foundry and furniture factory.

Both the Applebys and Laziers were of United Empire Loyalist stock. Richard Lazier was a direct descendant of Jacobus Lazier who had emigrated from Holland to New York state in 1680. In 1791, when the persecution of Loyalists in the United States was at its peak, Nicholas Lazier packed his family and moved to Prince Edward County. Richard Lazier, grandson of Nicholas, was born in Shannonville and later went into milling, not only at Milltown but Lonsdale as well.

Nathaniel Appleby was the son of Thomas Appleby of Duchess County, New York, who, like Nicholas Lazier, was forced from the United States during the Loyalist oppression.

Records cloud after 1880 for Milltown's businesses were then listed with those of Shannonville. Maps indicate that, by 1930, Milltown had declined drastically. In that year only seven buildings lined Main Street, few remained on Wellington Street and most of the other roads had disappeared.

In those intervening years Main Street had become the main highway between Toronto and Kingston—Provincial Highway 2—and many old stores and houses which had previously hugged the roadside were demolished to make way for the wider highway. As for the mills, the poor farming conditions and the depletion of wheat and timber supplies sealed their fate.

Today, Highway 2 is even wider and only a couple of Main Street buildings still stand. Newer homes have been added in recent years. While only a few original homes survive along Wellington Street, bushes and weeds are pushing through the foundations of the mills and the shops. Regan's iron foundry is used only for storage. The other roads have either disappeared completely or have become private lanes.

LONSDALE

Five miles upstream from Milltown, the Salmon River has cut a striking gorge into the limestone bedrock. It was a water power site in this gorge that attracted the mills which spawned the village of Lonsdale, architecturally the most appealing of Ontario's ghost towns.

On a small island in the river, in the 1830s, the Lazier brothers built a flour and saw, and, later, woollen mills. The woollen mill's proud reputation for the fine quality of its carding and cloth dressing was due in part to weavers Chris, Flora and Rebecca Frazer. To operate their flour mill, the Lazier brothers recruited from England one James McCullough who retained this position until his death in 1865. On the opposite side of the island, John Ross built a rival woollen mill but could not long compete.

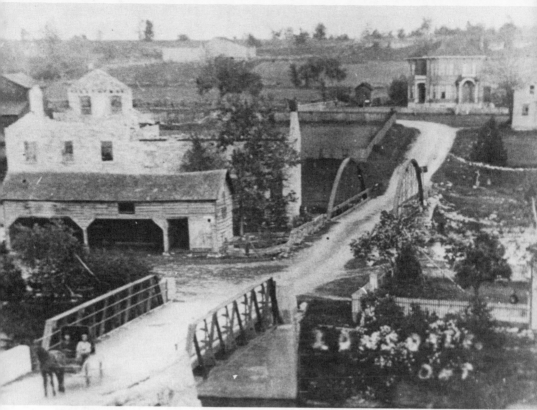

Bridge Street in Lonsdale, 1908 — abandonment has already begun.

Even before Lonsdale deteriorated to become a ghost town, a millpond belonging to one Meagher was believed to be haunted. To the fright of the villagers, the ghost of a young man who had drowned there appeared regularly. Finally they called in an exorcist who laid the wandering spirit to rest.

Business boomed. Lonsdale, in its early years, had three hotels (two lasting until the 1880s, that of Dennis Neelon until 1910), five black-smiths, two coopers, plus several carpenters, shoemakers and harness makers. John Bruin and Ben Haight established a carriage factory, P. Casey and Son, a wagon factory. The Casey operation continued until 1900, that of Bruin and Haight until the late 1890s, while the Lazier brothers' mill operated almost until the outbreak of the First World War. Richard Wildman and James McCullough operated general stores for several years.

In 1868 the Weslyan Methodists constructed a frame church, later replacing it with the beautiful limestone building which stands to this day. Lonsdale also boasted a school and a meeting hall.

The extensive village plot covered several acres of land on both rims of the valley. While on the south rim the plan consisted of only a few lanes heading off the main road, with only a few shops, on the north rim it comprised 10 blocks. Here most of the village was concentrated with

The former Lonsdale store, one of the village's many empty limestone buildings. (Photo, the author, 1975).

streets bearing such appropriate names as Rock Street, which followed a rocky ledge, and Bridge Street, which descended the steep valley wall and led past the mills in the valley bottom.

Discouraging soil conditions on the limestone plain drove away many farmers and doomed Lonsdale. By 1935, the only remaining businesses were the general store and blacksmith shop and these too disappeared shortly thereafter.

Ironically, the limestone which ruined the farmers provided Lonsdale with its most beautiful and lasting buildings. While most are abandoned, their durability has allowed them to remain as architectural treasures of rural Ontario's simple 19th century beauty. The school, church, store, hotel and mills, all made of local limestone, are now either vacant or used as residences.

Lonsdale's wooden buildings were less fortunate. While a few remain occupied and in fair repair, most have become vacant—sagging shells peering from behind lush lilac bushes. Many original frame buildings have vanished completely.

While Lonsdale's few remaining residents may question the ghost town category, the vacant lots, forlorn shells and vanished industries testify to a size and vitality long gone.

MILLS

When, in the 1790s the first waves of pioneer settlers reached Lake Ontario's shores west of Belleville, road transportation was unheard of. As access was only by lake or navigable river, the settlers ventured little beyond Lake Ontario's shoreline. But the vital need for mills could not be met at sites with no water power. As a result, a few pioneers

44

followed river valleys inland in search of millsites and soon crude roads linked the mills with the lakeshore. Later roads avoided the valleys and when newer villages appeared along them, the older mill villages vanished. Few in fact survived beyond 1850 or 1860.

Floods of 1870, 1880 and 1890 washed out many of the remaining mill dams and, with the decline in business, there was little incentive to rebuild.

DECKER HOLLOW

Through Hope township on Lake Ontario's shoreline, about 55 miles east of Toronto, flows the Ganaraska River. Its numerous water power sites attracted several early pioneer mills. At one such site, six miles north of Lake Ontario, John Decker arrived with sons Gilbert, Peter, Robert and Daniel and, in 1843, erected a grist mill with a sawmill attached to it. The mills soon attracted a store, tavern, blacksmith and several houses, and the name "Deckerville" was bestowed.

Decker operated the mill until 1870 and Dan Decker the tavern until 1867.

As long as traffic flowed along the Port Hope-Manvers road which angled across the township and through Deckerville, prosperity was assured. Those days, the middle years of the 19th century, were the palmy days of the village.

But, from the 1850s through the '70s, drastic changes occurred in transportation patterns and Deckerville's doom was sealed. The new Midland Railway, completed between Port Hope and Lindsay in 1857, and improved north-south roads reduced the traffic on the old Manvers road. Enjoying better access, the towns on these new routes drained away Deckerville's businesses.

Then came the floods. Before the 1870s, the forest cover had regulated the ground water so that rivers ran at a steady flow the year round. But once the trees were gone, rapid spring run-offs and dry summers created wide fluctuations in river flow. In the 1870s, the uncontrolled spring waters washed away many of the Ganaraska's old mill dams. Mill owners such as John Decker, operating by then at only a marginal profit, did not bother to rebuild. Subsequent flooding in the '80s and '90s, and again in the 1920s and '30s, washed away most traces of the old village.

Where the Manvers road skirted the valley rim and descended into the valley, cattle now graze, although the road alignment can still be traced through the farm woodlot. Where it crossed the river at Deckerville, it is scarcely discernable. Of John Decker's old village, no trace, save a few grassy mounds by the river, have survived the ravages of time and flood. Only the name has survived as Decker Hollow.

HOWELLS HOLLOW

Another early mill village, now long gone, developed near the headwaters of Duffins Creek, only a few miles northeast of Metropolitan Toronto, one-half mile south of Highway 7. Before the advent of roads, a Mr. Sicely in 1831 built a grist mill with a sawmill attached. Although a little village sprang up around it, no precise records of its shops and homes have survived.

Three years after Henry Howell bought the mill in 1833 the village had a post office and was named Brougham. For a time, Howell's grist mill was the only such facility in the district and the little village bristled with activity. Unfortunately for the village, road surveyors had passed it by and as roads improved, particularly the busy north-south Brock Road, businesses moved away to better locations. One such crossroads location was the junction of the Brock Road with what is now Highway 7. Known first as Bentley's Corners, it captured the Hollow's businesses, its post office and then its name, Brougham. Within 10 years Howells Hollow was a ghost town.

The new Brougham grew to be a major crossroads village and is today noted for its historic old brick hotels and fine period buildings. Howells Hollow, meanwhile, met an inglorious fate, degenerating to mere mounds in a barnyard and surrounded by gravel pits.

EMPIRE MILLS

Four miles north of Oshawa, on a small branch of the Oshawa Creek, there operated in 1835 the largest mills in the district, the woollen mills of Matheson and Ratcliffe. A far cry from the one- or two-man operations common in those days, the mills were manned by 50 workers brought especially from Lancashire and Yorkshire in England. They resided in a boarding house and in small cottages built for them. In 1850 Matheson and Ratcliffe sold the mills to the Empire Woollen Company. At its peak the village of Empire Mills boasted, in addition to the mills and dwellings, a church, store, school, wooden sidewalks and, by 1883, an electrical lighting system powered by the mill dam.

Then, in 1887, the railway passed through Markham, several miles to the west. Attracted by the advantages of rail access, the company moved. Nevertheless, the old mill struggled on under new ownership with a reduced work force of just 10 men until 1890 when floods washed away the dam. Paltry profits, outweighed by the costs of rebuilding, negated any incentive to rebuild and the village died. Today the cemetery is its only visible remnant.

But, there is new life in the area. The outer fringe of Oshawa's urban shadow has been steadily creeping up the old farm roads, bringing with it new homes and a vitality unseen since the days when Empire Mills was an important industrial village.

GERMAN MILLS

Nearly 200 years ago, settlers struggled northward along a forested trail, the forerunner of Yonge Street, into a wilderness remote from that cluster of log buildings on Lake Ontario which would later be called Toronto. One such band of 300 settlers, American emigres led by William Berczy, set their sights on a tract of land near the small Don River, about eight miles north of the lake and a mile and a half east of Yonge Street. Since there were no mills or shops closer than Toronto, the Berczy settlers built their own.

Using what little water power the site offered, the settlers erected a sawmill, flour mill, distillery, brewery, malt house, blacksmith shop and cooper shop as well as a number of private dwellings, and for two

The now quiet Don River Valley where once stood the busy old village of German Mills.

decades the village of German Mills prospered.

In 1799, only a few short years after the rise of the village, Berczy left in a huff over a patent dispute with the government. This had an apparently deflating effect on the village for, in 1805, the following advertisement appeared in a local newspaper: "...To be sold for payments of debts due to the creditors of William Berczy Esq. the Mills called the German Mills." The mills were purchased and operated by Captain Nolan of the 70th Regiment but the speculation was unsuccessful and, in 1828, the entire site was again offered for sale. As Dr. Scadding recalls in his book *Toronto of Old*: "...We remember about the year 1828 thinking the extensive cluster of buildings constituting the German Mills a rather impressive sight coming upon them suddenly in the midst of the woods in a deserted condition with their windows boarded up." Although the details of German Mills' decline—and death—have gone unrecorded, it can be reasonably surmised that once the Berczy settlers and others of their pioneer neighbours had cleared the forests, the regular flow of the millstream, scanty to begin with, dwindled and could no longer power the village's industries.

One hundred and fifty years have passed since Scadding's visit and little evidence remains of the forlorn scene which greeted him in the forest. Suburban sprawl has crept northward along the old farm roads and the fields have filled with extensive subdivisions. Although surrounded by the growing city, the little valley with its bubbling brook has, at least at the time of writing, escaped the sprawling asphalt and still retains traces of the old mill dam and reflects on days of a century and a half ago when the hum of an early pioneer village echoed through the primeval forest.

47

OVER THE DIVIDE:

While Ontario's lakeshore townships filled early, one great obstacle—that imposing divide of rolling, pine-covered sand hills known as "Oak Ridges Moraine"—impeded the northward road construction.

Spotty settlement preceded the roads. Irish settlers under the famous colonist, Peter Robinson, had sailed up the Otonabee River in 1828, circumventing the hills on the east and settled lands around Peterborough. Meanwhile, from the west, came settlers who had travelled north from York up Yonge Street over a low point in the ridge. But until the roads and railways mounted the hills from the south, settlement remained fairly scattered.

In the 1840s and '50s, keen rivalry between lakeshore ports to procure timber and grain from hinterland areas sparked a flurry of road and railroad construction. While the greatest rivalries were between the merchants of Cobourg and Port Hope, those in Belleville, Brighton, Colborne, Newcastle, Bowmanville and Oshawa sponsored roads northward through the gaps in the ridge and onto the plains behind.

The basis for villages north of the divide usually depended upon the availability of transportation facilities. Of the four ghost towns in this sub-chapter, Burnley and Bogart originated where major inland roads passed near millsites, Franklin on a railway line, and Port Hoover at a trans-shipment point on Lake Scugog. Their decline and disappearance coincided with changing modes of transportation, changes which meant the disappearance of the access that spawned and nurtured their early growth.

BOGART

In the 1840s and 1850s, the pioneer fringe of settlement flowed northward along the Tweed Road (now Highway 37) from Belleville to the area of Tweed and the shores of Stoco Lake. Along it trudged a member of one of North America's oldest and most respected Dutch families.

Abram Bogart was the great grandson of Jacob Bogart, a Dutch emigrant to Albany, New York, in 1689. Forced to flee the persecutions of the Loyalists which followed the American Revolution, the Bogarts arrived at Adolphuston, Ontario, near Kingston, in 1783. It was there that Abram was born. In 1853 Abram ventured northward to the banks of the Clare River, five miles east of modern-day Tweed, where he erected a saw and grist mill. Much in demand by pioneer farmers, the mills attracted enough business for Bogart to add a general store. He was then granted a post office which carried his name.

The mills attracted other rural businesses and, by 1864, swelled to a village with two shoemakers, two builders, a wagon maker, cooper, cabinetmaker and a blacksmith named Peter Sherbon.

By 1884 the village had grown and changed. The Murphy family acquired most of Bogart's operations: Frank and Mike Murphy the flour and sawmill, James Murphy the general store. The population had reached 100 and to its list of functions the village added a school, Methodist Church, cheese factory and another sawmill. Most of these

The former General Store and blacksmith shop at Bogart (1976).

industries and institutions developed along two short side streets off the main road, on either side of the river.

By 1900 Bogart's palmy days had passed. Its industries suffered from the decline in wheat, timber and dairy products and from the shifts in transportation routes. Soon its only businesses were James Murphy's store, Thrasher's blacksmith shop and the Rodger brothers' cabinet shop.

Today few of Bogart's old buildings survive. The general store and blacksmith shop, across the road from each other, are no longer used as such and the school stands abandoned. Gone are Bogart's old mills, although the mill ponds have survived. Of most of the other village buildings, only grassy lots and foundations remain. Much of the land around Bogart which once fostered a prosperous farming community now supports only marginal part-time farms, the victims of stony soils and poor market access.

BURNLEY

Another well-travelled settlement road in the 1840s and 50s was that leading from Port Hope on Lake Ontario to Hastings on the Trent River, now provincial Highway 45. Just south of modern-day Fenella in Haldimand township, Northumberland County, about the mid-way point on the road, the rushing waters of Mill Creek crossed the route. Along this creek pioneer settlers sought millsites and erected much needed saw and grist mills.

Pioneer mill builder R.H. Grimshaw found a power site five miles east of the road and, by 1860, had in operation grist and sawmills. R. Pringle, who owned considerable land at the site, recognized the potential for village development and subdivided his property into

49

The quaint old general store at Burnley (1976).

village lots which, in a short time, sprouted several homes and businesses. Among the first were John Donohue's Burnley Hotel, William Lawlor's store and, in the '80s, Alex MacDonald's cheese factory. There were in addition a blacksmith, shoemaker, Roman Catholic Church, separate school, and community hall. Burnley grew and prospered and by the turn of the century its population peaked at 125. During these years stages departed three times per week along the Colborne Road south to the larger towns of Colborne on Lake Ontario and Castleton, half-way between.

The 20-year period between 1910 and 1930 witnessed Burnley's demise. A changing agricultural economy which saw the decline in grain and cheese production cost Burnley its major industries, except for the general store which J.R. Downs operated for a few years thereafter. By 1940, only nine buildings, including the church and school, remained.

Today, the old community hall and store are abandoned. The church went in the '60s, leaving only fence and foundation, while the large old cheese factory has been converted to a stylish private residence. Of the mills and hotel, of the other homes and businesses, only grassy lots remain. The new owners of the old store and adjacent lots tell of discovering a number of old bottles while cleaning the hotel site behind the store. Unfortunately, their plans to demolish the store will destroy a fine example of early Ontario's gingerbread style of building adornment.

FRANKLIN

While the most popular method used by Lake Ontario's port villages to trap hinterland trade was road building, a few of the more zealous communities embarked on railway building schemes. Port Hope and Colborne, perhaps because of their proximity to one another, entered into a particularly keen rivalry, each building railways northward—Port Hope completing the "Midland Railway" to Lindsay in 1857-8, while Colborne's interests pushed a railway over a long causeway across Rice Lake and on to Peterborough. The Colborne line lasted only a few years until Rice Lake's waves washed away the embankments. The Port Hope line, however, operated for several decades.

Stations and villages appeared along the line. One station, five miles north of modern-day Bethany on Highway 7A, Manvers township, was Franklin, appropriately named after an early sawmill owner named Frank Lyn. Here, amid a gentle and prosperous farming country, the station attracted two stores, blacksmith, post office, grist mill, grain elevator, cattle yards, the Franklin House Hotel, run by James Lytle, and a dozen homes.

"Hec" Tripp, whose grandfather at one time ran the Franklin store, noted of Franklin's heydays in *The Rolling Hills* by Mrs. R.N. Carr: "At the turn of the century my paternal grandfather was post-master and general merchant in the small village of Franklin, Ontario, a hamlet that is no longer recorded on the map. Before Granddad's time the place supported a dozen homes, a blacksmith shop and two taverns. The next era saw the taverns go out and more houses come in and the Grand Trunk Railway ran daily except Sunday from Port Hope to Lindsay. It was a most exciting chore when as small kids we were allowed to carry the mail bags down to the train and hoist them up to the mail clerk and in return may(be) get several bags to lug back to the Post Office, which was tucked away in one corner of the store."

Franklin's village plan included half a dozen streets, of which only three were ever used, and 32 lots.

In 1912 a branch of the CPR was built just two miles to the west and the ensuing competition meant the end of Franklin. Sixteen years later the older money-losing railway closed and Franklin began to fade. By 1940, only the church and eight other buildings remained; by 1960 the one-time village was down to just four occupied buildings. Today even these have gone and Franklin is nothing more than a dirt road lined with foundations and overgrown yards.

Sections of the old Midland Railway have been converted to a roadway and provide a scenic drive between the pretty rural villages of Omemee and Bethany.

PORT HOOVER

Port Hoover was unusual in that it was an "inland" port. On the swampy northern shores of the artificial Lake Scugog, 40 miles northeast of Toronto, it developed as a transfer point for timber and farm produce bound for Port Darlington (now part of Bowmanville), on Lake Ontario. The goods crossed on schooners to Caesarea, on Scugog's southern shore, and then south along the Scugog Road. Steamers also linked Port Hoover with the town of Lindsay, located a few miles to the northeast on the banks of the Scugog River.

Port Hoover's life was short. In the late 1850s, when Dan Hoover built a store and saw and shingle mill on the isthmus in the lake, the govern-

Port Hoover's sister village, Caesarea, shown here, trans-shipped produce, ferried from Port Hoover, on to the Scugog Road which wound its way to the export centres on Lake Ontario.

ment installed a post office and the fledgling village seemed destined to have a promising future. E. Veitch opened the Steamboat Hotel, a few artisans moved in and a number of private dwellings appeared. Port Hoover's main street ran straight down the centre of the isthmus while short side streets ran east to Hoover's mill and west to the wharf.

Despite this promising beginning, by 1880 Port Hoover had become a scene of neglect. By then better roads and railways linked Port Perry on Scugog's western shores with the larger Lake Ontario town of Oshawa and movement of goods followed this more efficient route. A sawmill at Port Hoover operated for a time but it, too, soon disappeared.

Today a recent cottage subdivision rings the point of land where Port Hoover once stood—a strange location considering the swampy and stagnant nature of the waters in this part of Lake Scugog. Of the original buildings on the old main street only the former store and hotel still stand, now used as residences. The others have faded away into fields or have been obliterated by the construction of the subdivision. In spite of the new construction, the view from the point is still pleasing and one which the residents of this one-time inland port must have enjoyed.

IN THE SHADOW OF THE CITY:

Regardless how odd it seems to think of ghost towns within a city's urban shadow, many villages within Toronto's call lost their functions long before Toronto began its outward sprawl. During the 19th century the fertile farmlands northwest of Toronto were thickly populated and villages appeared at most major crossroads. As the century closed, most lost all their functions and many of their residents to the larger towns. Several also lost nearly all of their citizens. Research has placed the number of abandoned or nearly abandoned villages in this

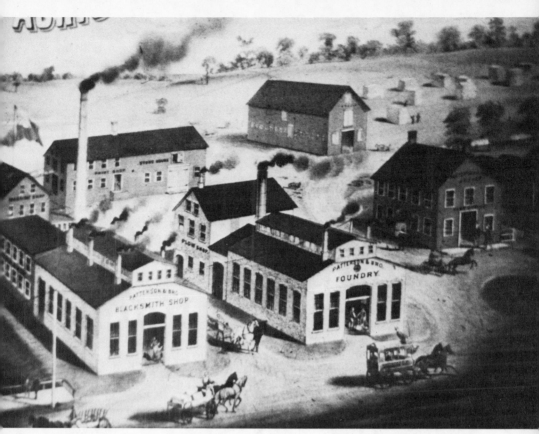

Patterson's foundry during its years of operation (photo by the author, from a painting hanging in the Redelmeier farm office).

area at 60. The largest and most interesting are the ghost towns of Patterson, Grahamsville, Stanley Mills, Ballycroy and Keenansville. Patterson sits near the fringe of the sprawl, one mile west of Yonge Street at Richmond Hill, and just five miles north of Toronto's urban fringe. Grahamsville and Stanley Mills both developed on what is now Airport Road: Grahamsville, two miles north of Toronto's northwestern fringe at Malton, and Stanley Mills, six miles farther north beyond site of the city, but as much within its shadow as the others. Keenansville and Ballycroy, neighbouring ghost towns, occupy the northern fringes of Toronto's commutershed, some miles north of Stanley Mills.

PATTERSON
The efforts of one or two individuals to develop from nothing a large and profitable industry deserve praiseworthy pages in the history of this province.

Peter Patterson and his brothers were early settlers who had followed Yonge Street 15 miles north from tiny Toronto to their plot one mile west of what is now Richmond Hill. An enterprising family, the Pattersons developed Canada's largest factory of farm implements from a sawmill on their farm. Ontario's farm industry was booming and the market was ripe for such an enterprise.

To accommodate their large labour force, the Pattersons built a village of 25 cottages and a boarding house. 1867 found 60 men working at the foundry, in apparent contentment, for, as one worker wrote (as quoted in the Richmond Hill *Liberal*, August 11, 1976): "The boss seems to be a nice man and the boys are the jolliest set I ever came across." William Snowden operated the boarding house, charging only $3 per week; Peter Patterson operated the general store and was the village's postmaster.

In 1871 the village population reached 500, while, at the foundry, the labour force of 200 included 23 machinists, 17 carpenters, 21 labourers, 9 blacksmiths, 10 moulders and 4 painters.

A description of the operation appeared in the Richmond Hill *Liberal* of 1885: "From the ground floor where the rough material is first handled to the upper storey where all the machinery is finished and neatly painted, every article passes from one room to another with the precision of clockwork... Four teams of heavy horses are kept constantly busy drawing their machines to the railroad station." While self-binders became the most popular product, spring tooth harrows and cultivators also sold well.

The Pattersons developed a unique expertise in the art of tempering steel and developed a thriving sideline by selling it to other foundries throughout the province.

In 1885 rumours swept the "Patch," as the village had become known, that the foundry was to close, that the factory which was the life-blood of the village and surrounding community was to relocate in Woodstock. The editor of the *Liberal* urged that $17,000 be spent on a railway spur to encourage the Pattersons to stay and save the area from economic disaster. But the citizens of Woodstock spoke money too. By a vote of 669 to 50, they favoured giving the Patterson brothers a $35,000 incentive to relocate in their village. That decision sealed the "Patch's" fate and in 1886 the factory went, piece by piece, to its new site. 1887 saw Patterson a deserted village.

Years later Peter Patterson's son, John, returned to the old farm, rehabilitated the buildings and began raising sheep and cattle. Following the younger Patterson's death in 1940, Willy Redelmeier purchased the farm and passed it on to sons Ernest and Francis who operate it to this day.

The boarding house and all save three of the cottages have gone. The original foundry now serves as a barn for the Redelmeier's cattle and the driving shed still stands much as it did 100 years ago. Mounds of earth mark the site of the old store and post office.

Although Toronto's skyline lurks on the horizon, this area remains a prosperous farming community which has more than fully recovered from its economic "disaster" of nearly a century ago when the "Patch" went from boom to bust.

GRAHAMSVILLE

One hundred and 25 years ago the "Sixth Line" of Peel county was a long way from its current name, "Airport Road". One of those main

Grahamsville, a sketch representing the appearance of the southeast corner as it may have appeared prior to 1880 (based on contemporary descriptions).

Little other than this cemetary and building remain at Grahamsville (1977).

north-south arteries well-travelled by pioneer settlers, it became the backbone for a string of villages. While most lost their businesses in the closing years of the 19th century, many retained a number of residences. Grahamsville, however, lost everything. In recent years Toronto's urban sprawl has crept up Airport Road and the outer fringe of urbanization lurks just two miles away.

In 1850 Toronto was still a long day's journey by stage, a trip costing 50 cents each way, and Grahamsville was nearing its zenith as a crossroads service town for the area's many prosperous farmers.

Grahamsville's beginning dates back to 1819 when pioneer Thomas Graham obtained a tavern licence and turned this intersection into a regional centre. Since the Graham family owned all the land on which the village grew, the new post office was placed in Graham's general store and named Grahamsville in 1852.

Other businesses gathered at the corner and the village grew rapidly. In the 1870s the *Illustrated Atlas of the County of Peel* noted: "The village now contains 2 churches, Methodist and English, with good schools convenient. It has one store and post office kept by Peter Lamphien (a misspelling, actually "Lamphier"); a blacksmith shop, John Cook; and a hotel called the 'Magnet' by William Hunwick." The visitor could also have noted John Watson's extensive manufactory of carriages, wagons and ploughs, a building later to become the Agricultural Building for the fair grounds, William Clifton's shoe emporium and such other enterprises as a tailor, another blacksmith and wagon maker, Masonic Hall and Orange Hall. The town also numbered among its residents three doctors, one of whom, Dr. T.G. Phillips, was directly descended from T.B. Phillips who, with the Grahams, had settled and pioneered in the area. Dr. Phillips served the community for more than 30 years.

Grahamsville's fall from prosperity began on a disastrous night in October of 1880. On that night a fire swept away one-quarter of the town. Then, again, on March 24, 1882, another fire devastated much of what the first fire missed. The Brampton *Conservator* of March 31, 1882, reported: "...Fire broke out on the 24th which consumed a large frame building the under part of which was used as a blacksmith shop and the upper part a public hall, also a small frame building in which the blacksmith resided and another one-and-a-half-storey frame building the under part used for election purposes and the upper part as a masonic hall. The blacksmith had no insurance, Mr. Lamphier's property was partly insured. The buildings all belonged to Lamphier."

If the area was so prosperous, why is it that no one rebuilt that which was burned? The answer lay in the changes which, in the 1880s, were affecting all of rural Ontario.

By 1880 the railways had removed industrial and retail importance from the old corner villages and placed them in the railway towns. Then, too, technological advance had dated the small village businesses and only larger operations could turn a profit.

Within 20 years, Grahamsville's population slid from the 200 of that fateful year to a mere 35 in 1908 when Peter Lamphier finally closed his general store. A few residents survived for a number of years and a gas station opened on the site of the old hotel. The church was sold in 1902 but the old cemetery commemorates many original pioneers and includes the weathered headstone of pioneer founder Thomas Graham. Of the other buildings, only lot lines, mounds of earth and scattered lumber remain from the days when the crossroads village community was a busy focus for farmers from miles around.

STANLEY MILLS

In the middle of the last century quite a string of villages appeared along the sixth line north of Grahamsville: Woodhill (now completely asphalted by a major intersection), Stanley Mills, Tullamore, Sandhill, Mono Road, Caledon East (these last four still possess a number of old buildings), and Sleswick (a tiny hamlet now vanished).

Since Peel County's flat countryside possesses very few regular creeks and streams, those that did provide water power potential attracted sawmills and grist mills during the early stages of settlement.

In 1825 Thomas Burrell erected the first mill in the Hollow, as it was first called. Samuel Stanley in 1831 erected a log mill and in 1832 became postmaster. From that year the village was known as Stanley Mills. Burrell nevertheless became the village's chief industrialist, erecting a grist mill, distillery, sawmill, tannery, blacksmith, store, tavern and warehouse. He was known widely as "Squire." His granddaughter, the late Mrs. J.P. Thurston, wrote from Bloomfield, New York: "Grandfather Burrell...in time succeeded in building up quite a village. It not only included the Hollow proper but the valley running halfway to the 7th line. In this valley he had a gristmill and distillery...on the 6th line in the Hollow he had a store, blacksmith, saw mill, grain, hides and wool wholesale, hotel and saw mill and other buildings (houses etc.)... At one time he employed 60 men for whom grandma Burrell had to do the cooking. The men went to work at 2 a.m., breakfast was served at 4 a.m."

As the surrounding farm population grew and required more services, more businesses opened in the village and, by 1864, Stanley Mills' population had climbed to 200. A contemporary business directory listed three blacksmiths, a harness maker, tanner, carriage and wagon maker and carpenter in addition to the two grist mills. George Dale had opened the Union Hotel for liquid refreshment while true spiritual sustenance was available at the new Wesleyan-Methodist Church. The Balfour family ran a general store, the daughters operating a small millinery on the second floor. Several years later George Ward opened a second store. Most of the village's buildings straddled the sixth line road where it dipped in and out of the two gullies. A few other buildings lined two short side streets which ran eastward from the main road along each rim of the larger gully. In 1850 a small brick Methodist Church was added.

Stanley's mill eventually passed into the hands of William Alderson. Following a fire which destroyed the old log structure, Alderson erected a two-and-a-half storey mill with two run of stone. The low flow of the creek necessitated an auxiliary engine.

For reasons never clear, Stanley Mills had declined dramatically by 1870. Only Alderson's mill and the general store remained. Alderson's mill was still going strong in 1873 and employed several hands but when it closed a few years later much of what remained died.

In 1884 the Brampton *Conservator* reported that one resident, Robert Blackburn, had been negotiating with the village mayor to lay a sidewalk along the main street "as the streets are very muddy". Time has erased any record as to whether the walk was built.

A few original buildings have remained standing to this day—the former shops now used as garages or storage sheds, the homes still occupied. But, for the most part, today's motorists speed along the wide, paved Airport Road, north to cottage country or south to Toronto, oblivious that this series of shaded gullies once witnessed the activity of an early pioneer mill town.

BALLYCROY

One of Ontario's most scenic ghost towns, Ballycroy, high in the rugged Albion Hills 40 miles northwest of Toronto, commands an enchanting

A rare photo of old Ballycroy Mill, 1936 (from an article in the Toronto TELEGRAM, 1936).

Ruins of the mill dam at Ballycroy.

The quiet remains of Ballycroy, within sound of two busy highways.

view of the twisting Credit River valley mantled with the green foliage of a young forest. Water power from this river gave Ballycroy its initial impetus for growth.

In 1819 Samuel Beatty erected a much-needed sawmill and, soon after, John Leslier a grist mill. Attracted by the business generated by the mills, other shops soon appeared. By 1864, John McLelland and Peter Small had opened hotels and general stores and Don Skelly a blacksmith shop. By the mid '70s the village boasted shoemakers, harness makers, a blacksmith and a population of over 150. William and Sam Beatty opened a carding mill near the original sawmill while Henry Bracken took over the grist mill. Mike Feheley became the hotel's new owner.

Ballycroy was fortunate in her situation. The village enjoyed both water power advantages and location at a busy road junction (now Highways 50 and 9).

The main roads from both Orangeville and Toronto formerly met in the centre of Ballycroy.

Most of Ballycroy's buildings gathered about the valley rim along the Toronto road. Several also lined the Orangeville Road which wound down the steep valley wall towards the mills nestled in the gully.

Dominating the village heart was Peter Small's massive inn. It was a large building housing a hotel, post office, tailor, telegraph office and grocer. Dances were frequently held there. A contemporary account describes the scene: "The ballroom was notable for its splendour... enormous piles of eatables were laid out on the tables...dances lasted all night and far into the next day. It was usually decorous enough at first but was apt to degenerate rapidly as liquor circulated and not infrequently broke up in wild free-for-alls."

On the night of April 29, 1875, tragedy struck the village. A fire destroyed the hotel, blacksmith shop, wood-working shop, three dwellings, McMaster's tavern and a large shed. Three girls staying in the hotel were trapped in their rooms and died. Arson was suspected but never proved.

Frequent visitors to the area were the legendary Black Donnellys, who were accused of many crimes around Lucan, Ontario, including that of arson.

In 1878 a new store opened: "Mr. William Cook begs to inform his old customers that he has returned to Ballycroy and is working in the shop adjoining Messrs. Cobean and McLelland store where will be found a large and well assorted stock of tweeds and worsted coatings—New York Fashion."

Although for many years Feheley's hotel, McLelland's store, Beatty's and McElwain's mills and Irwin's blacksmith shop continued as Ballycroy's mainstays, the new century witnessed their disappearance—victims of the shift to rising railway towns. Of Ballycroy's many early industries, only the grist mill survived the dawn of the 20th century and celebrated its 115th birthday in 1936.

As businesses and families moved to better opportunities in larger towns, Ballycroy's buildings gradually fell vacant. When the Toronto road became a provincial highway and was straightened to by-pass the village, the mill road fell into disuse. The Orangeville Road also became a provincial highway and the once important junction was suddenly a backwater.

Today only foundations, shells and a few old buildings bespeak the Ballycroy of old. The former general store now displays antiques, while three other original residences are still occupied. The old mill road had remained virtually unaltered since the last century and as such is a unique vestige of pioneer Ontario. Along it lie several foundations, mounds, overgrown lots, and a vacant dwelling. Although much of the scenic land around Ballycroy has passed from farming to country estates and nearly desecrated the beauty of the area, more than the gaudy materialism of Toronto's rich will be required to diminish the beauty of the Albion Hills which enfold the ghost town of Ballycroy.

KEENANSVILLE

Only a few buildings on the flat plains north of the Albion Hills mark the site of Keenansville, former township capital and bustling mill town of the last century.

Acquiring its name from the pioneering Keenan family, the village of Keenansville originated at a water power site on Bailey Creek in the southwest corner of Adjala township and quickly attracted a large number of businesses. By 1866 this bustling town of 300 boasted two hotels, including Thomas Morrow's Ontario House, a general store, two blacksmith shops, three shoe emporiums, four wagon factories, a sawmill and woollen mill.

From his general store George Hughes published a weekly newspaper known first as the Simcoe *Observer* and later as the Cardwell *Sentinel* in which he regaled his 1,000 subscribers with frequent reprimands of local bureaucratic bungling. Of the poor repair of the Bailey Creek bridge, Hughes warned: "Will the Keenansville pathmaster see to the dangerous state of the bridge... If not, we'll see to him." And of the local mail delivery came this familiar criticism "...It takes 3 days for a letter to travel from Mono Mills to Keenansville, a distance of 11 miles which it ought to reach in a few hours. Will somebody see to it."

(Left) One of Keenansville's ghosts—recently burned down. (Right) One of Keenansville's old stores, now demolished.

Prices in the Hughes' store would make today's shopper envious, for, as he advertised in the Cardwell *Sentinel,* sugar was 12 pounds for a dollar, cotton 7 cents a yard, and shirts 50 cents each.

Paramount among Keenansville's industries was the Brown brothers' woollen mill, run by Thomas, John and Joseph Brown and employing three weavers, four carders, five framers and a spinner. It continued as the community's mainstay for over 40 years until it closed just prior to the First World War. The Browns offered a wide range of clothing: wool flannels, union flannels, domestic and horse blankets, shirts, winceys and tweeds, while a suit made to order would cost $12 to $15. The Browns had their share of difficulties, however, Hughes' paper reporting a dam-burst and a robbery within a year.

The centre of social life was Thomas Moore's Ontario House Hotel. Balls and dinners were common and marked each year's several festive occasions. When the successes of the local temperance movement forced the end of liquor sales, the Ontario House Hotel became unprofitable to operate and soon closed its doors.

Before temperance won the day, Keenansville must have been a boisterous place. Hughes frequently chastised the young and the not-so-young for their "notorious...and unseemly brawls". To restore order, Keenansville hired a police force of two constables. After the hotel closed, the tiny constabulary was disbanded.

Considering its geographical disadvantages well away from travelled roads and from rail lines, Keenansville achieved a considerable size and tenacity.

The changing economics of 19th century Ontario soon caught up with the village and, one by one, the businesses closed or moved to more economical locations. Only two stayed. The general store which George Morrow bought and operated until the First World War, and John Cahoon's wagon and furniture factory survived the economic changes of the period.

The Brown brothers' dam is still visible on Bailey Creek as are the mounds of earth which mark the remains of the old woollen mill itself. Empty buildings, foundations, and lilac bushes mark the former business section. An old shop now sits forlorn and vacant in a farmer's

61

field while the hotel, now a private residence, and three other original buidings are still occupied. One building, a dilapidated shell until it burned, contained as recently as 1975 pieces of original furniture, all the worse for wear after long exposure to ravages of weather and vandalism. Today's quiet rural scene scarcely reflects the bustling town that was Keenansville in the days of small-town Ontario.

TWIXT ERIE AND ONTARIO:

Early in the 19th century the pioneer fringe broke through the forest barrier between Lakes Erie and Ontario. As throughout Ontario water power sites were focal points for the first villages, Balls Falls developed in the 1830s on the brink of the Niagara Escarpment where a series of water falls provided ample water power, while Sinclairville developed a little later at a water power site on nearby Chippewa Creek.

Railways reached the region in the 1850s, long before the great stands of pine and oak had been cleared. Along the lines small stations and sidings for timber shipment often attracted steam-powered sawmills. Around some mills small villages grew. Cook Station was one such place where a sizable mill workers' community thrived for a short time.

The close of the 19th century saw winds of change sweep the area. Timber became depleted as farms expanded. With the tree-cover gone, millstreams dried up and industries found larger towns more to their liking. As these factors caused most country villages to dwindle, they caused Balls Falls, Cook Station and Sinclairville to die.

BALLS FALLS

The Niagara Peninsula is defined by Lake Erie on the south, Lake Ontario on the north and the Niagara River on the east and is divided by towering cliffs of the Niagara Escarpment.

Over these cliffs a series of rivers cascade to the fruitlands below. Most such cascades attracted mills. One site, now known as Balls Falls, two miles south of modern-day Jordan on Highway 8, consisted of two attractive waterfalls with ample water power potential. In the 1830s the community which grew here seemed destined to become a major centre in the Niagara Peninsula. Today it is a quiet picnic area, the old grist mill a museum.

The story of Balls Falls, or Glen Elgin as it was first called, dates to 1807. George and John Ball, returning from military service with Butler's Rangers, were granted a plot of land totalling 1,200 acres at the site on Twenty Mile Creek. To serve the needs of the growing farming community, the brothers, in 1812, erected a grist mill at the lower of the two falls and, shortly after, saw and woollen mills at the upper falls. The mills were large even for their day. The two-storey grist mill used four run of stone to grind wheat hauled as far as 20 miles. The Ball brothers exported much of their wheat through Jordan Harbour at the mouth of Twenty Mile Creek to Montreal and Liverpool.

The woollen mill was a "skyscraper" in its day—five storeys high. The women who worked the eight looms turned out a variety of knit-wear including light and heavy kerseys, cassimers, satinets, tweeds

A team of oxen in the village of Balls Falls.

The grist mill at Balls Falls before the turn of the century.

63

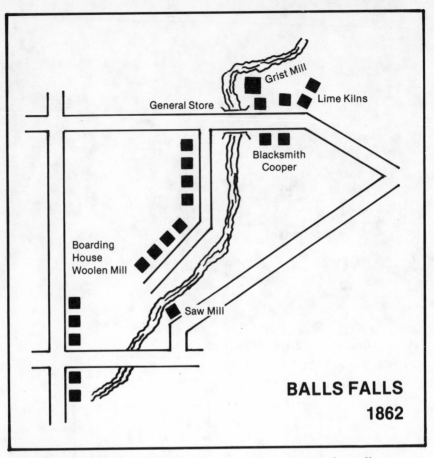

General Store
Grist Mill
Lime Kilns
Blacksmith
Cooper
Boarding
House
Woolen Mill
Saw Mill

**BALLS FALLS
1862**

and flannels. They resided in a boarding house next to the mill.

Lured by the promising future which Glen Elgin seemed to offer, many other businessmen arrived. In the 1830s and 40s, the town had, in addition to the saw, flour and woollen mills, a barrel maker (the barrels were used to ship the flour), a blacksmith, two lime kilns which used to advantage the nearby limestone outcroppings, a general store and several dwellings. The village was concentrated between the two falls, several buildings facing the river, others facing the cross-valley road.

Then came the railway, the great maker of towns through which it passed, and the breaker of towns which it by-passed...and in 1850 the Great Western Railway by-passed Balls Falls. Using the flatlands below the cliffs, the railway gave much easier market access to the communities near it, and the industries at Balls Falls could not compete. Within 30 years all but the grist mill had closed. It struggled on until 1912 when lack of business forced it, too, to shut down. Balls Falls had died.

The site today is a popular picnic park. Although most of the original village buildings have long since disappeared, the grist mill still stands. Other survivors include the large brick Ball home, which also housed

Only two buildings and a line of trees mark the former centre of Cook Station.

the general store, and remnants of the lime kilns in the face of the cliffs. The river, however, did not survive, its waters backed up for much of the year behind a control dam.

To complement the pioneer atmosphere of the site, the park authorities have moved in pioneer log cabins from elsewhere. The mill, now a museum, displays, along with many artifacts of early Ontario, the life and death of this pioneer mill town.

COOK STATION

Shortly after the completion of the Buffalo-Port Huron Railroad in 1852 through a still forested hinterland, a number of mills were built near the stations to facilitate timber export. At Cook Station, on Concession 3 of Seneca township, Haldimand County, a substantial mill workers' village developed containing 75 houses by 1877. Many Irish immigrants who had worked on the construction of the railway settled in Cook Station. One Irishman, Bill Winters, ran one of the Cook Station stores for a number of years.

Cook Station depended upon a single industry, the cutting and export of timber. When the supply of timber was finally exhausted, the mills closed and the village faded from the maps.

Little remains of Cook Station to testify to its earlier importance. Only two buildings, shaded by a row of maples, indicate the town's former core. In the cluttered fields and along the road lie the scarcely discernible foundations of many old buildings. Only an imaginative eye could now "reconstruct" the Cook Station of those early days when lumber was king.

SINCLAIRVILLE

The quiet intersection of County Road 34 and the Wentworth-Norfolk county line road beside Chippewa Creek gives no modern hint that here existed in the 19th century the country village of Sinclairville.

A water power site on Chippewa Creek was the chief attraction for early settlers and Sinclairville was soon a busy milling and service village. At its zenith, in the 1880s, it comprised two stores, two blacksmith shops, two sawmills, a shingle mill, shoemaker, two hotels, weaving shop, Temperance Hall, a Methodist Church and several homes.

The hotels were known as the Crawford House and Wilson Hotel. John Austin was the first blacksmith, the second, William Rattenbury. John C. Hewitt bought the latter's shop and specialized in making plows. Hewitt also reputedly manufactured forceps with which he practised a sideline dentistry with few repeat customers—little wonder. John Robinson was the village shoemaker whose special "Diggers" had a reputation for longevity. Robinson's wife and daughter operated a weaving ship making both carpets and wall hangings.

The village had three mills: a water-powered sawmill owned by the Baron family, a steam sawmill built by Robert Hewitt, and a shingle mill. The Hewitt mill once blew up, killing one Joe Phenix.

A driving force behind the development of Sinclairville was the Hewitt family. As the Ontario Directory for 1888 indicates, no less than five members of the Hewitt family operated various village industries including the sawmill, blacksmith shop, shoe shop, carpentry shop and a veterinary service. James Wilson was another major figure in the village, as indeed postmasters generally were in those days, for he faithfully kept the mails flowing from his hotel and general store for over 30 years until the post office closed in 1915.

Even though today's modern country roads have digressed from the old street pattern, the former roads are still traceable. Along them the old shops and houses are little more than grassy mounds. Only three original buildings remain in use while a handsome brick structure replaced the old frame church.   ●

4

ONTARIO WESTERN PLAINS

Southwestern Ontario is one of Canada's most productive food baskets. This area, described as a peninsula between Lakes Erie and Huron, west of the Grand River and south of Goderich, was, in its original state, anything but "plains". Rather, the first pioneers into the area encountered great stands of pine, park-like oak plains, and dense hardwood forests. However, so fertile were the soils that the farmers quickly denuded the woodland to the present vista of field and pasture which indeed resembles a near treeless plain.

Despite prior settlements near Windsor and along the Lake Erie shoreline, only after the 1812 war was the region surveyed.

Settlement at first occurred under ambitious colonization schemes. That of Colonel. Thos. Talbot was the first. In the 1820s he undertook to colonize a broad tract of land south of modern-day London with serious, hard-working Scottish immigrants. Another was that of the Canada Company. Through the forests of what was then called the "Huron Tract" between modern-day Galt and Goderich, now the counties of Huron and Perth, the Company opened settlement roads and lured thousands of farmers. The Huron Tract possessed the deep fertile soils which ensured a prosperous and enduring farming community, while the large rivers which incised the plains guaranteed water power and easy transportation.

The middle portion of the plain, today's counties of Lambton and Middlesex, felt a slower but steady frontier of individual settlement rather than colonization. Between 1830-1850, Scottish, English and Irish emigrants, escaping the famines, oppressive landlords and economic depressions of the British Isles, gradually filled the area.

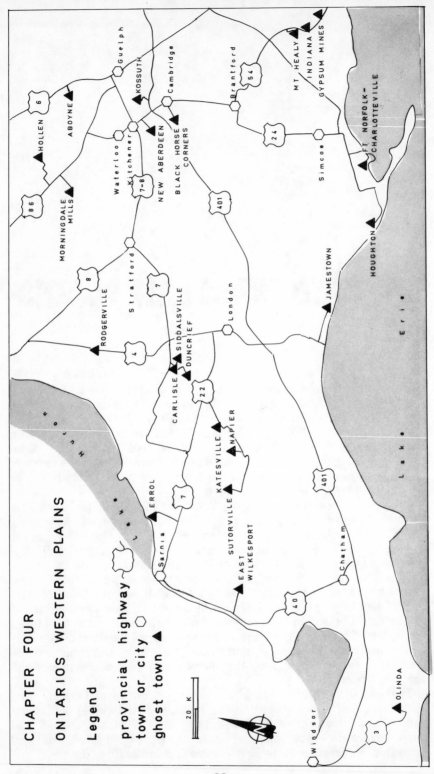

CHAPTER FOUR

ONTARIOS WESTERN PLAINS

Legend

provincial highway ⬡
town or city ◯
ghost town ▲

20 K

With few areas excepted, Ontario's western plains were, by 1853, occupied by busy pioneer farmers. Prosperity prevailed. Industrial villages sprang up at millsites on the rivers, farmers' businesses clustered at major road junctions or at stopping places along the settlement roads. As early as the 1830s and 40s, most of the ghost towns of this area were booming villages.

Many grew to sizeable proportions. Then, with the railway age, between 1850 and 1880, the pattern changed drastically. Millsites lost their attraction and often their water power and railway towns became the focus for newer and larger industries. New technologies and economies of scale dated one-man industries. By 1900 many villages, once bustling with industrial activity, contained little more than a general store and village blacksmith. With the inauguration of rural postal delivery around 1914, and with the disappearance of horse-power in the 20s and 30s, even these vanished.

THE UPPER GRAND VALLEY:

In an unimpressive swamp northwest of modern-day Orangeville, the mighty Grand River rises. In its upper reaches the tiny river meanders through swamps and flat farmlands reclaimed from swamps. After picking up countless creeks and streams, the Grand River flows strongly and steadily towards Fergus and Elora where it has carved into the limestone bedrock a spectacular gorge. Beyond the mouth of the gorge, the Grand enters rolling fertile farmlands, the home of the traditional Mennonite farmers where the cities of Kitchener and Waterloo have grown.

Settlement of the upper Grand Valley dates from the influx of Mennonite refugees from the United States in the 1790s. They were followed in the 1830s and '40s by German and British settlers who settled around Kitchener. Scottish immigrants settled the Fergus and Elora area around the 1830s-50s. Areas north and west of Kitchener received settlement after the 1850s.

KOSSUTH

Although Kitchener is one of Canada's fastest growing cities, her suburban fringes have yet to creep across the little ghost village of Kossuth, which straddles the quiet intersection of Waterloo County Roads 30 and 31, 3 miles north of Hespeler and 5 miles east of Kitchener.

A hundred and forty years ago, when these grain lands were still partly forested and the road a dirt track, Kossuth was born as a bustling pioneer stopping place.

An influx of workers constructing the Grand Trunk Railway gave the little village a brief boom. Located as it was, half-way between the rail-head and the supply of limestone, Cossel's Hotel provided frequent overnight accommodation and respite for the weary teamsters.

By 1871 the village had grown to a population of 150 and acquired a number of other businesses including a blacksmith, weaver, tailor, cabinet makers, shoemakers and several carpenters. Swiss-born Joseph Zyrd for a number of years operated a match-making factory which, because of the sulphuric odour of the brimstone, was well known throughout the area. Of the half-dozen local girls who toiled at the factory the Waterloo Historical Society *Annual Report* of 1930 had this comment: "The girls employed in making these matches were often very beautiful, it is said, but the brimstone odour of their garments prompted thoughts of the place of the damned." Few were the beaus who would walk these ladies home from work. Chris Prange manufactured pumps while John Groh operated the store and post office. Stages departed Kossuth twice weekly for Breslau and Preston.

As the century drew to a close and a changing economy doomed many country villages, Kossuth dwindled. By 1896 only two businesses remained. Henry Sohrt, shoemaker by trade, had taken over the general store while Joseph Smuck, the blacksmith, operated the hotel. When the First World War drew heavily upon Canada's supply of construction materials, the old hotel was dismantled so that its bricks could be used elsewhere. Shortly afterwards Henry Sohrt closed his store.

Today only a pair of original residences rise over the grain fields while weedy yards have intruded upon the sites of former businesses and residences.

BLACK HORSE CORNERS

Pioneer Ontario contained an uncountable number of crossroad hamlets with the minimum range of businesses required by the area's farmers: a hotel, store, and blacksmith. Seldom did the village limits extend beyond the four corners of a country intersection.

Because these four-corner hamlets were small and left few reminders of their former glory, they are of little interest to the ghost town hunter. Black Horse Corners is an exception. Despite its small size, this old four-corner settlement enjoyed a notoriety in its day, and is still fondly revered by Waterloo County history buffs.

In the 1850s and 1860s, when homesteading was giving way to full-time farming, the beverages of the Black Horse tavern, five miles west of modern-day Galt, drew farmers from far and wide. Like many hotels today, serving beverages was the old inn's mainstay as it only had five rooms. But for reasons unrecorded the old tavern changed hands no less than 6 times in 22 years; Nelson Newcombe survived the longest, 12 years as proprietor.

In its heyday, Black Horse Corners boasted a wagonmaker, shoemaker, and blacksmith and a handful of small houses. The creek which flowed through the village contained a sufficient flow of water to power a tannery run by one Eccles. Erected in 1843, it later became a fulling mill. Jacob Bechtel later acquired it for the manufacturing of pumps and shingles.

The year 1875 marked the beginning of the end for Black Horse Corners. In that year the old Black Horse Inn burned to the ground and was never rebuilt.

When tree clearing lowered the water tables, the creek could no longer provide water power. Gradually the businesses moved away and Black Horse Corners vanished from the maps. Although the little village has been a favourite subject for local writers, there are, other than lot lines and a few mounds of earth that mark old building sites, no vestiges to remind today's visitor of this once lively little village.

NEW ABERDEEN

The clearing of forests doomed many a pioneer mill town. Where mill towns relied heavily on a steady supply of local wood and water power from a small stream, the end often came early. Once the forests were cleared nothing remained to retain the moisture in the soil. The water level lowered, drying small streams. Thus lacking both water power and supplies the mills closed and the villages dwindled.

New Aberdeen, a once bustling pioneer mill town, nestled in what is now only a weedy gulch beside the old Huron Wagon Road on the southwest fringe of Kitchener's ever-expanding suburbs. It was born in the manner of many mill towns. An early settler, after acquiring a tract of unbroken land with water privileges, erected a mill to serve the pioneers.

George Davidson was that pioneer and his mill soon became the focus for several other pioneer businesses. North of the dusty, rutted Huron Road he constructed a dam and redirected the water through a mill race to his mill south of the road. By 1851 the site had become a bustling nucleus of pioneer industries including a blacksmith, a carpenter, wagonmaker, tailor and shoemaker, as well as two coopers, two weavers and, in succeeding years, two additional mills. Davidson, in addition to his mill, ran a general store. Amos Bent's hotel provided rest and repast for weary travellers using the daily Huron Road stages.

The town grew quickly. In the 6 years between 1851 and 1857 its

New Aberdeen was in the 1850s a busy up-and-coming village. This sketch, based on information from a map published in the 1850s, represents the author's impression of New Aberdeen's appearance in those heady days of growth.

71

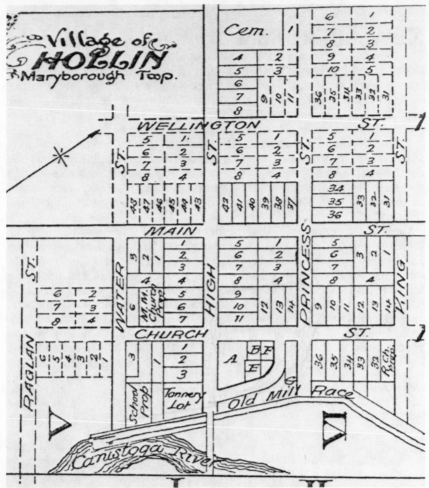

Town Plan of the village of "Hollin" circa 1906 (from the Illustrated Historical Atlas of the County of Wellington, 1906).

population rose from 125 to 200. Anticipating a boom, land-owners surveyed a townsite comprising 10 streets and over 160 lots. Most, however, remained unsold.

Nevertheless, New Aberdeen of the 1860s was a bustle of industry and commerce, her mills, stores, hotel and shops nestled in the valley bottom, her dwellings straddling the road on the valley's rim and slopes.

By 1871 many changes had occurred. A busy new railroad by-passed the village and created the boom-towns of Kitchener, Waterloo, Preston and Hespeler, magnets for New Aberdeen's industries.

By 1871 only the general store, sawmill and wagon maker remained. Soon after, New Aberdeen was still, its businesses gone and only three homes left.

New Aberdeen today is just a grassy meadow. The little stream

Once a busy corner, Hollen's main intersection today is quiet.

carries but an occasional trickle and the mill ponds are silted. The Huron Road is now a paved suburban artery while George and Queen Streets are farm lanes, and once-busy Margaret Street, which lead to the mill, is virtually untraceable. Only two old residences remain.

Quiet for nearly a hundred years, the old site will soon change. As the valley lies in the shadow of Kitchener, a fast-growing city, it is not surprising that a major developer owns the entire area. Soon asphalt and endless rows of look-alike houses will dominate the little valley where once nestled this early pioneer mill town.

HOLLEN

The vanished village of Hollen on the banks of the new Conestoga Reservoir exemplifies more than most the devastating impact that railways had on early Ontario farming towns.

In 1850 Hugh Hollingshead recognized the water power potential of the Conestoga River, three miles southwest of Drayton in Maryboro township, and set about building grist and shingle mills. His friend, Sam Robertson, arrived at the same time and opened a general store and post office. Attracted by the fertile soils, pioneers were at this time streaming into the area, the woods echoing to the ring of the axe.

Hollingshead, anticipating the boom, laid out a large village plot of nearly 150 lots. They quickly filled and in a mere 20 years Hollen had boomed from forest to a thriving village of 400. Mills, factories and shops trooped in: Joe Billings set up a carding mill, Mannel and sons a tannery and shoe emporium, James Dickson took over the shingle mill and Chuck Hadnel, the grist mill. There were two inns, including the well-known Western Hotel, two general stores, coopers, harnessmakers, cabinet-makers, tailors, dressmakers, blacksmiths, a cheese factory and brickyard. The village also boasted a school, two churches, a doctor and a music teacher.

Stagecoaches bounced along rugged country roads from Hollen to the nearby villages of Yatton, Floradale, Drayton and Stirton for fares of 30-50 cents, and to faraway Elmira, Waterloo and Kitchener.

Hollen basked in prosperity for a number of years as an important service town for the growing farm community. Irwin and Burnham described the Hollen of 1867 as having "excellent facilities for manufacturing, unlimited water privileges and is in the midst of a fertile country."

However, when the railway system stretched its tentacles into western Ontario, Hollen's future turned bleak. One line by-passed her well to the north and east, another well to the south and west. As the newer steam mills required no water power, a riverside site was no longer an advantage. In the face of new technologies, the town of Hollen began to dwindle.

Owing to the size of the town and the tenacity of its citizens, Hollen refused to die overnight. For some years after the unsettling impacts of the railway, Potter and Reid kept the grist mill grinding; John Patterson, and later Sam Rodgers, kept the sawmill buzzing. The blacksmith shop and general store both served the community for several years as did George Wilson's hotel—at least until the local liquor option forbade the selling of alcohol in the township. Finally, in 1914, when the post office closed, Hollen had lost all industries and businesses. However, the school continued to educate farmers' children until 1944 and the United Church kept open its doors until 1960. The Methodist Church had left Hollen in 1915 for a new home in nearby Creekbank.

Sadly, however, Hollen had become a ghost town. Hazel Mack, writing in 1948, described the village as totally vacated although a number of buildings were still in good repair.

Since the river had not entirely lost its appeal, nor its ability to flood, the Grand Valley Conservation Authority in 1958 completed a dam to control floods and provide a much needed recreational outlet for the citizens of nearby communities.

Gradually life crept back into old Hollen. Had the old Methodist Church remained, it would abut a row of new cottages; the Conestoga Bible School complex was erected on the old mill lot and the old school came tumbling down to be replaced by a large lakeside residence.

Thus, although the ghost town explorer will find considerable life around Hollen, he will not be disappointed for many relics remain of the Hollen that was. Traces of old Princess Street run through a shrubby field and a number of overgrown foundations, including that of the general store, still abound. Still standing as proud reminders of Hollen's heyday are the blacksmith shop and wagon factory, both disused, and a small number of old village homes.

ABOYNE

Pioneer villages were often keenly competitive. Several would develop within close proximity to each other. Nine miles north of Guelph, along a four-mile stretch of the Grand River, five hopeful communities competed with each other. Fergus was the easternmost, then, within hailing distance of each other, Kinnettles, Aboyne, Elora and Salem. All had promising beginnings. In 1870 Aboyne was in the forefront of the

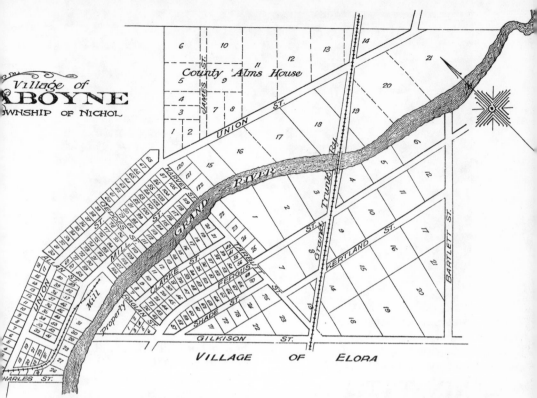

Town plan of the village of Aboyne as it appeared in 1906 (from ILLUSTRATED HISTORICAL ATLAS OF THE COUNTRY OF WELLINGTON).

five-village rivalry as the many water power sites on the turbulent Grand encouraged the construction of several mills.

The grist, oat and flax mills of James Henneberry Company provided Aboyne's industrial base. A large operation for the period, it employed a dozen workers and required a special railway spur line from the main line at Fergus. Robert Young's tannery and John Moore's hotel comprised the village's other major businesses. Such was the optimism of these heady days that Aboyne's landowners laid out, on both sides of the river, a substantial town plan of 120 lots. Speculators and settlers quickly bought up the lots but the bubble burst before most could build on them. Because Fergus and Elora possessed road and rail advantages, new businesses rallied to these towns and Aboyne dwindled. Soon after the turn of the century her residents had gone and her mills closed.

Fergus and Elora have continued to flourish as industrial and commercial villages; Salem lost all her industries but retained her residences; Aboyne and Kinnettles vanished.

Today, the Aboyne site possesses interesting vestiges of its former existence. The shells of the mills provide a scene of forlorn limestone walls rising from the rocky river banks. Of the old village side streets, Allan, Mill and Gilkison are still traceable; the others have lost to the

Mill ruins on the Grand River at Aboyne.

intrusion of grass and weeds. A few newer homes have been built by commuters to the nearby cities of Guelph and Kitchener.

KINNETTLES

In more optimistic times a town was planned on the banks of the Grand River between Aboyne and Fergus and quite a few lots were laid out. This city-to-be had a promising future and many prospective residents bought lots. But when the competition between the five Grand River villages proved to be too keen Kinettles disappeared almost as soon as it began. Although some old foundations remained visible until the late 1940s a new subdivision has since sprawled across the Kinnettles site, obliterating all evidence of the fledgling village.

MORNINGDALE MILLS

Six miles south of Hollen and one mile north of Millbank, on Perth County Road 7 lies the site of the old mill village of Morningdale Mills. Here on the headwaters of the Nith River, a tributary of the Grand where early mills once ground out grist from wheat, a small park now draws local residents for weekend picnics.

Although Morningdale Mills was never large, it was a typical pioneer mill town.

More than anything else the enterprise of early settler John Nicklin was responsible for Morningdale Mills' development. His grist mill was quite an imposing structure—four floors high with a run of 3 stones operating from a 30-horse-power engine. He, with his sons, opened a general store and for a time ran a tavern. John Gordon, shoemaker, later assumed operation of the tavern while Dave Nicklin managed the store. At various times the village was home to two shoemakers, two carpenters, a tinsmith and James Wright's shingle factory.

In 1864 Nicklin had attempted to sell his mill for $1,000 but failed to attract any buyers even though in those days Morningdale Mills was an important place. *The Illustrated Historical Atlas of the County of Perth* reported: "Morningdale Mills, about 2 miles from Millbank, is of some importance, containing as it does a store, mill, and post office".

But this pioneer village, for reasons frequently repeated—a dried millstream and competition from larger villages—died before the dawn of the 20th century.

Nothing of the old village remains. Even the old road which once twisted through the small gully has been replaced by a modern bridge. A solitary log cabin, removed from a location elsewhere, does invoke an image of by-gone days as do the very real horse-drawn buggies of the Old Order Mennonites who farm the area.

THE LOWER GRAND VALLEY:

Before the heady days of railway building and road improvements, Ontario looked to its rivers for transportation. Most rivers were small and flowed irregularly, only their estuaries being useful for boating. The larger rivers, however, inspired a flurry of canal building. In fact, the 1820s and 30s were known as the canal age and gave birth to such canals as the Rideau, Trent, St. Lawrence and Welland, all of which remain in heavy use. This period also gave birth to smaller canals, many now forgotten, such as the Grand River Canal.

Initial efforts by Major Jones and Absolom Shade of Galt to bring barge traffic to the Grand River were foiled by spring floods and irregular flow. However, in 1832, after flow was regulated by construction of a feeder line to the newly opened Welland Canal, a few miles east, construction of a canal on the Grand River became feasible and the Grand River Navigation Company was formed.

After obtaining a charter in 1832 the company quickly constructed a 13-mile-long, 8-lock canal which linked Brantford with the head of navigable water on the Grand and thence with Lake Erie. Opportunities at the locks for loading and unloading the river barges attracted industries and businesses and soon a string of lock villages, including Newport, Middleport, York, Indiana and Cainsville appeared along the canal. Mt. Healy, while not at a lock, benefitted from the transportation improvement afforded by the canal. Other Grand River towns of Cayuga, Caledonia and Brantford, which predate the canal, enjoyed a boom when the system opened.

MT. HEALY

Mt. Healy, a half-mile from the nearest lock station at York, grew on the strength of one of Haldimand County's more enterprising and respected pioneer businessmen, John Donaldson.

Born in England in 1795, Donaldson migrated to Upper Canada and purchased a triangular riverside parcel of land where the Grand River narrows to rush around Youngs Island. Recognizing the water power potential of the rapids, Donaldson wasted little time in erecting saw and grist mills. The need for such facilities by the ever-increasing pioneer population was immediate. Donaldson's enterprises prospered

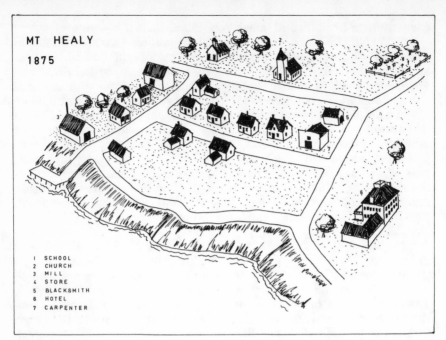

MT HEALY
1875

1 SCHOOL
2 CHURCH
3 MILL
4 STORE
5 BLACKSMITH
6 HOTEL
7 CARPENTER

Contemporary sketch of the Dochstader Hotel in Mt. Healy, 1862, (from Tremaine's ATLAS OF HALDIMAND COUNTY 1862).

and his respect spread. A contemporary observer commented: "Even before 1850, Mt. Healey, which owed its existence to the enterprise of John Donaldson, was doing a lot of business with a saw mill, plaster mill, blacksmith, carriage maker and hotel." To this we might add the grist mill.

Donaldson's sawmill was large and modern. He had equipped it with the newly-invented upright saw. His source of timber was close at hand—the lofty white pines which grew in abundance along the sandy banks of the river. These, once cut into sawlogs, were shipped via the canal to a variety of Great Lakes ports.

Donaldson's plaster mill similarly took its raw material from the banks of the Grand. Gypsum layers normally occur far below the surface of the land, but here the forces of the Grand River had eroded away the overburden, exposing the gypsum at several locations along the riverbank. Barges hauled the gypsum to Donaldson's mill whence the refined plaster was exported via the canal.

To many of the mill hands, home was Henry Dochstader's handsome brick hotel. Built at a bend in the shore road, it commanded a grand view of the river.

By 1869 the village had grown to 150 persons and had added a brick school, a Presbyterian church (non-denominational at first) where Rev. James Bates once preached, and a sturdy drill hall where, following the Fenian raids of 1867, Captain William Mussen, owner of a distillery at nearby Indiana, commanded the "Number Eight" Company, Mt. Healy. The village consisted of five streets, the centre of which contained the village homes.

In 1866 John Donaldson died. His three sons, with the help of their brother-in-law, A.W. Thompson, ably continued to operate the three mills, general store and post office until the close of the century.

By then the Grand River Canal had long been closed and the fortunes of the river towns were swiftly ebbing. In 1908 the fine old sawmill was silenced forever. The only remaining industry was the extraction of gypsum from the Mt. Healy mine.

Now the dams are gone and the Grand River once more rushes unobstructed around Youngs Island. Of the wharves and mills, no traces remain. The school, church and drill hall have all vanished; the cemetery lies overgrown and forlorn. Of all the original shops and houses, only one house remains. The rest are rows of grassy mounds in a forgotten field. However, the old Dochstader Hotel now stands grander than ever, having been renovated by recent owner, David Olson.

INDIANA

Indiana was founded by David Thompson, a major shareholder in the Grand River Navigation Company.

In 1832 he had purchased 1200 acres at a water power site and built a dam and grist mill. Thomas Lester followed in 1838, purchasing a large tract of land adjacent to Thompson's, and there opened a sawmill and a pail factory. Thus, even before the canal arrived, Indiana possessed a nucleus of industrial activity.

When the canal arrived and Indiana became the site of the fifth lock station, industrial growth accelerated.

W.H. Smith observed that the Indiana of 1846 was "A small village... pleasantly situated on the Grand River... It contains 120 inhabitants and a Catholic Church...one grist mill, two saw mills, distillery, two stores, two taverns, one pail factory, one blacksmith, two shoemakers, one cabinetmaker, one tailor, one wagon maker."

Indiana's town plan included 117 lots, 7 mill sites and 10 streets, the busiest being Colborne and York Streets, the shore road, and Robinson Street leading to the back concessions. Many of the lots were quickly

Town plan of the village of Indiana circa 1880 (from ILLUSTRATED HISTORIC- AL ATLAS OF THE COUNTY OF HALDIMAND).

snapped up and the population soared to 300. In 1870 Indiana hummed with no less than 30 industries or trades including three hotels, five stores, three mills and three factories. There were also two churches and a school.

The Mussen brothers and James Kirkland both operated distilleries, Thompson and Lester the grist and sawmills. From his pail factory, Lester shipped 50 dozen pails to Hamilton each week. While a Mr. Young and his family hand-operated a little swing bridge over the narrow canal, a 500-foot bridge spanned the Grand River. Jacob Wigg's daily stages linked Indiana with the riverside towns of Cayuga, York and Caledonia at fares as low as 10 cents.

Indiana was strongly Irish and Catholic as the family names testify: Pat Farrel, owner of the Anglo-American Hotel, Alex Kinnear, Justice of the Peace, Charles McKenna, merchant, James Mclory, blacksmith, Peter McMullen, shipowner, and Miles Finlan, owner of the Indiana Hotel.

Soon the inevitable railways began steaming across the countryside, moving goods faster and cheaper, and the canal closed forever. With the decline in the fortunes of the Grand River Canal went the fortunes of many of the villages. In 1878 Beldon noted in his Haldimand County Atlas that Indiana had become "an old village which grew into brief importance while the old Navigation company existed but dropped into decay and delapidation (sic) when those temporary causes of prosperity were removed."

By 1890 Indiana scarcely resembled the industrial town it once had been. Of her commercial ventures, there remained only Pat Cannon's hotel, Stephenson's store and sawmill, and the grist mill of the man who first founded the settlement, David Thompson. By 1900 these too

Contemporary sketch of Indiana grist mill and saw mills on the Grand River Canal circa 1862 (source: TREMAINE'S ATLAS OF HALDIMAND COUNTY, 1862).

One of Indiana's former main roads is now just a private lane.

were gone. The population of Indiana between 1860 and 1900 shrank from 300 to a mere 25.

The old York and Colborne Streets have become provincial Highway 54, an attractive riverside drive. But speeding motorists may easily overlook old Indiana for only two large houses stand among the weedy lots which line the old main street. Markham Street, down which teams of horses hauled wheat to the grist mill, is now a dead-end lane with only the former post office and a private residence. Here the riverbank is steep and overgrown. A long flight of cracked concrete steps lead through the bush to the rotting timbers which mark the grist mill site. Where barges and skiffs once waited in the old lock, young trees now grow and the canal, long drained, is a grassy pasture.

81

GYPSUM MINES

Not all the activity of the Grand River depended upon the canal as the brief rise to fame of Gypsum Mines attests.

William Holmes, in 1822, was the first to discover gypsum in the Grand River area. On his deposit near Paris he built a mill to grind the gypsum as fertilizer. Fourteen deposits along the banks of the Grand were subsequently discovered and mined.

Of these, four outcropped on a bend of the river three miles south of Cayuga. On this bend, the village of Gypsum Mines sprang up as a home for miners and millers and as a headquarters for the Grand River Plaster Company and the Alabastine Company. Its population quickly rose to 100 and production from the mines and mills soon topped 550 million tons. Between 1875 and 1878 three mills began grinding plaster. In 1886 and 1891 the respective companies added calcining plants to their operations. The deposits, however, were small, none exceeding four feet in depth and were soon exhausted. One by one the mines closed. In 1911 the Toronto Plaster Company took over the Grand River Company operations and was the last to operate.

Gypsum Mines village at first consisted almost entirely of accommodation for miners. It later attracted sawmills, general stores, and blacksmiths. Nearly all the buildings lined either the shore road or the riverbank, a few hundred feet distant. Two sawmills, owned by Joe Evans and R.A. Sutor respectively, began cutting lumber around 1900 and operated for several years. General stores were run at various times by Stockton, Rostuck, and the Walton brothers but had vanished by 1914, as had the two blacksmiths. While the mines were active a stage operated daily to Cayuga.

When the mines closed, the village died. Today, only a row of shrubby mounds and weed-covered lots bear mute testimony to the only village in Ontario to depend exclusively upon gypsum mining.

OLD ERIE:

With the victory of the Americans in their revolutionary struggle, a stream of United Empire Loyalist refugees began crossing the border along the Niagara River into Canada. From there they spread to Lake Erie's shoreline townships. Since the lake was the only "highway," the earliest villages were those at the river-mouth harbours and, upstream, at the heads of navigable water where mills were usually erected and quickly became focal points for village growth. Boarding houses and cottages accommodated mill hands, while the business carried on at the mill attracted other shops and such additional industries as distilleries or flour mills.

As crude roads inched inland from the harbours, settlement followed. The flat sandy plains which characterize the area, although undesirable for general farming, yielded considerable lucrative pine stands. To tap this source of revenue, settlers eagerly moved on to their farm lots and several mills sprang up on the small streams which meandered through the sandy plains. Once the lofty pines were cut, the soils, useless for farming, drove farmers away. With the forest cover gone, the millstreams dried up leaving mills idle and mill towns vacant.

JAMESTOWN

Jamestown developed at a water power site on Catfish Creek just a few miles upstream from the harbour town of Port Bruce. There James Chrysler, a wealthy merchant from the nearby town of St. Thomas, built a distillery, grist and sawmills, and a store and gave Jamestown its name. Barges shuttled back and forth between Port Bruce and Jamestown carrying lumber out and supplies in, and the town became quite an active community.

One seasoned traveller, geographer W.H. Smith, visited Jamestown in 1846 and described it as "a small settlement near the south-east corner of the township Yarmouth on Catfish Creek, about one mile from Lake Erie, (which) contains a grist and saw mill, distillery, and about 10 houses".

But, alas, for Jamestown, transportation emphasis shifted from water to road. Her decline was swift. Thirty-five years later little remained. In 1879, in his *Atlas of Elgin County*, Beldon recounted: "Jamestown, a flourishing little place in 1840, has gone to decay."

The valley of Catfish Creek has remained quiet and picturesque, a serene river valley where only farms break the stillness. Except for traces of old roads, no vestige of the milling activity which once filled the valley has survived to this day.

CHARLOTTEVILLE AND FT. NORFOLK

National defence was the rationale for much of the early settlement in the Lake Erie vicinity. Sabre-rattling by the newly-independent United States spurred then governor of Upper Canada, John Graves Simcoe, to undertake the development of a system of self-sufficient garrisons, which he called "bridgeheads," each having a military population and a settlement of farmers to provide food and, when needed, additional manpower.

Simcoe deemed Long Point on Lake Erie to have excellent potential for settlement. In 1793 he exclaimed, "At slight expense (Long Point could) be strongly fortified and which from its position opposite Presque Isle and its vicinity to Ft. Erie is admirably calculated to become the naval arsenal on Lake Erie."

Many of Simcoe's bridgeheads went on to become sizeable towns and villages and the military routes which linked them became Ontario's modern highways. But when Charlotteville, the designated bridgehead and district capital, and Fort Norfolk, the military garrison, had fulfilled their functions, they dwindled, died, and passed into the pages of history, leaving little other than rusting cannon and cellar holes.

In 1795, however, the Charlotteville settlement was destined for greatness. Simcoe envisaged a shipyard in the harbour created by a long spit of land jutting into Lake Erie and, on a bluff overlooking the harbour, Fort Norfolk and a townsite to be named Charlotteville after Charlotte, the wife of King George III.

In 1800 the district of London was created and Charlotteville named its capital. The ambitious town plot included 48 one-acre lots set about a large square.

Slowly the town began to take form. In 1802 Job Loder, a local carpenter, constructed a temporary log courthouse and, in 1803, a log jail. In 1804 Loder completed a permanent two-storey courthouse. Although only three lots in the village had actually been granted up to that time, considerable building was proceeding in Charlotteville's vicinity. By 1812 there were four grist mills, three saw mills, three distilleries, three tanneries, four shoemakers, two tailors, three blacksmiths, four carpenters, two stores, two hatters, one potter, one physician, two churches, four schools and two public buildings.

The outbreak of war in 1812 accelerated the military construction. In 1813 the shipyard was ready and in that year launched its first ship, the *Lady Prevost*. At Fort Norfolk, construction of a blockhouse large enough to accommodate 300-500 men was speeded up. Although the fort was spared direct combat, its very presence served to discourage the American advances along the Lake Erie shoreline which had begun with a raid on Port Dover, only a few miles to the east. However, the destruction of the Port Dover mills by the Americans deprived Fort Norfolk of sufficient provisions and the blockhouse remained unfinished.

Then the war ended and, in 1815, the inland town of Vittoria became the new capital of London District. Thus both the military and administrative functions left Charlotteville and Fort Norfolk. Industries of the day usually required a water power site and Charlotteville, high on a bluff and far removed from any rivers or streams, failed to attract any industry which would have provided a mainstay.

With no reason to live, Charlotteville died. By 1823, it was described as a complete ruin. The village was resurveyed in 1853 by James Black but to no avail. In 1898 all that could be found of the early fort and capital of London District were a few cellar holes and some rusting 12-pound cannons.

Today the site is part of a golf course with little other than an historic plaque to indicate the former existence of the village. Controversy swirls as to whether the plaque should remain. Some government reports have suggested that since the settlement may not have been as large as earlier thought, the plaque should be removed. This would be unfortunate. The small size of the settlement does not diminish the role that Simcoe's bridgeheads played, not only in the military protection of Upper Canada, but in the pattern of settlement as well.

HOUGHTON

Ontario was still young when hardy pioneers trekked into Norfolk County's flat sandy shorelands. Several stopping places along the shoreline road provided respite for the travellers. Businesses soon gathered at these nodes, creating, by the 1840s and '50s, a string of villages which included Clear Creek, Jacksonburg, Hemlock and Houghton.

Houghton attracted more functions than the others and then

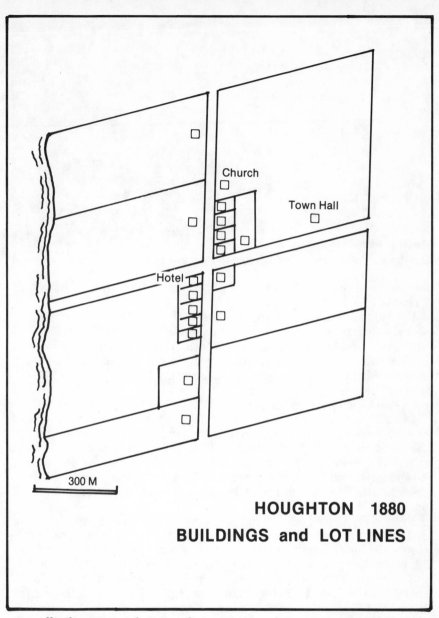

Church

Town Hall

Hotel

300 M

HOUGHTON 1880

BUILDINGS and LOT LINES

virtually disappeared. Its early name, Houghton Centre, reflected its early role as the area's political and educational capital. The township council chambers were located here as was the district school superintendent and three of his teachers.

Because of the heavy demand for the oak timber which proliferated on the sand plains, Houghton buzzed steadily with the noise of three sawmills. It became a busy town. There were also shoemakers, blacksmiths, carpenters, tanners, general labourers, even sailors. The Baptists built a solid brick church which, along with the school and town hall, ensured Houghton's primacy among its neighbours. A stage

Handsome homes once lined Houghton's main street—hotel in foreground.

left the hotel daily for Pt. Burwell at 50 cents a fare, and Pt. Rowan at 75 cents.

Houghton's early entrepreneurs were often called upon to manage several businesses at one time. For example, hotel owners Jeremy Hill and David and James Jackson also operated busy sawmills. While the Hills eventually moved away, the Jackson family expanded into wagon making (Abraham) and cheese manufacturing (Samuel), while Martha Jackson assumed management of the hotel. The Gates family also operated a general store and sawmill.

In 1870 the population peaked at 350, but even then the winds of change were blowing. The victory of the temperance movement forced the hotel to abandon liquor sales. With less and less traffic on the roads, the hotel finally closed its doors. Soon the great oak stands disappeared and the sawmills too fell silent. Since the town had lost its original attractions, the remaining businessmen, discouraged, moved on.

Even today the old lakeshore road, now paved, is but lightly travelled and presents one of Ontario's more attractive drives. The white clapboard hotel stands yet at the intersection of county roads 42 and 28, a photographer's delight. But of the many original residences only three remain. Fields of tall blowing cornstalks seem ready to invade the roadsides once lined by Houghton's other proud homes. Although the town hall fell into disuse, becoming a zinc-covered shed, the red brick church has survived the ravages of time and constitutes the only surviving function at a place that once played an important role on the shores of Lake Erie.

ROADS TO LONDON:

The winds sweep unimpeded across the flat treeless farmlands north of London where farms are large and prosperous.

Before the coming of paved roads and cars, even before the railroads, farm service towns were many, home to the millers, smithies and suppliers upon whom the farmers relied.

SIDDALSVILLE

Siddalsville dates from 1820 when John Siddal built the area's first grist mill on what came to be Siddal's Creek, later Nairn Creek, some three and one-half miles east of Ailsa Craig and one-half mile south of present-day Highway 7.

The site soon attracted other businesses and, although small, the resulting village contained all services essential to the farmer. In the 1860s there were, in addition to Siddal's mill, a blacksmith shop and a general store where the farmers conducted their business before retiring to Grif Phillips' tavern for a bit of liquid refreshment.

When, in 1867, the old mill burned to the ground, Siddal, then 90 years old, finally retired. This tragedy did no damage to Siddal's zest for life for he lived on for several years afterward.

Only a few grassy foundations in a field testify to the existence of Siddalsville. But if the traveller searches carefully, he may still find the old mill dam and a mound which, in 1828, was John Siddal's proud new mill.

CARLISLE

Siddalsville's next door neighbour, Carlisle, developed one-half mile downstream and was the younger of the two villages. However, it rapidly outgrew John Siddal's old village.

Contemporary directories placed its 1850-60 population at 1,000 but this may have been an exaggeration as most later sources quoted just a little over 200. Nevertheless it achieved a considerable size with an impressive list of businesses: R. Lambert and sons operated a woollen mill, James Wescott a sawmill and later a grist mill, and Lionel Shipley, a flour mill. Thirty other businesses included blacksmiths, shoemakers, builders, tanners, tailors, wagon makers, masons, dressmakers, saddlers and candle makers. There also were three general stores and

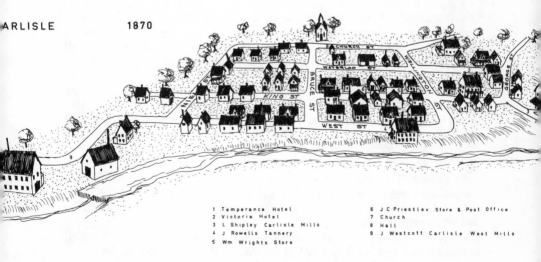

CARLISLE   1870

1 Temperance Hotel
2 Victoria Hotel
3 L Shipley Carlisle Mills
4 J Rowells Tannery
5 Wm Wrights Store
6 J C Priestley Store & Post Office
7 Church
8 Hall
9 J Westcott Carlisle West Mills

Joe Haskett's hotel. The town had churches, doctors, a school and a stage leaving Haskett's hotel daily. But when the London Huron and Bruce Railway built a line just a few miles to the east, most businessmen moved away to such railway towns as Denfield and Ilderton. By the late 1880s, only Haskett's hotel, Wescott's sawmill and Shipley's flour mill continued in business along with the general store and blacksmith. By the outbreak of the first war, only the store remained.

A large town plan existed in more optimistic days. Indeed, many lots sprouted homes or shops. But with the demise of the village most fell vacant, her many streets untravelled. Several lots have recently been sold to a dozen London commuters and a flurry of house construction is underway and must be reminiscent of the feverish growth of the original Carlisle over a century ago. Amid the new, one may yet find the old and the beautiful. Haskett's handsome old Victorian hotel has been beautifully preserved while five other fine old residences have retained the simple beauty of their Victorian style. The remaining sections of the once extensive town are no more than grassy yards beside overgrown roads.

DUNCRIEF

Just four miles south of Carlisle, lot 18 Concession 10 of Lobo township, 2 miles northeast of County Roads 16 and 17, lie the silent remains of Duncrief. Here, in 1835, on land originally owned by Joseph and Robert Charlton, Jeremiah Robson built a sawmill and the little mill village was born. In 1840 Joseph Charlton erected a flour mill and with his sons operated it until 1886. In that year J.C. Shipley, who had worked his father's mill in Carlisle, purchased the Charlton mill but sold it just four years later to J.B. Pethram. Pethram had come from Napier, another ghost town described later in this chapter.

"The mill was a great centre in the community," Dr. S.E. Charlton noted in his *History of Charlton Family*: "Wheat was brought from the country round about and ground into flour, teamed and sold at Ailsa Craig. Sometimes the dam would break and there would be a great rallying of neighbours and relations to restore it. Boys would be there and how we did enjoy it when meal time came, and we were ushered into the spacious dining room where the tables were laden with all sorts of food comprising roast beef, roast chicken, plum pudding and pies and cakes of all description."

In 1895 the mill burned. When the people of the community learned that Pethram had no money to rebuild, the residents immediately undertook a successful canvassing to raise the funds. A slight controversy followed construction, C.R. Charlton noting in *Duncrief 1835-1920*, "Some criticism was indulged in over a dance which was held in the mill after its completion... The wisdom of such an entertainment is a question of education and opinion and in this particular case the young men had all worked hard helping to erect the mill and it would have been small potatoes to have refused them an evening's enjoyment."

Twelve years after Pethram's sale to J.G. Kirby, in 1908, the mill wheel ground to a final stop when the dam washed out for the last time.

The old Duncrief General Store circa 1885.

James Barnes opened the village's first store and post office in 1862. Four owners and 41 years later the store and post office closed. Of these, S.T. Barclay operated it the longest, 30 years, from 1880 to 1910.

The village also watched the coming and going of several blacksmiths, the steadiest being Thomas Oliver who operated the smithy from 1870-1890 and again from 1900-1905. Many of today's farmers still possess cow chains forged by Oliver's bellows.

The white frame church, however, did not survive beyond 1895 as the village's newcomers preferred to retain religious affiliations elsewhere.

Little remains of old Duncrief where the quiet, seldom used country road twists through the small gully. Of the original buildings, only one forlorn old structure stands sagging beside the road, and only mounds of earth and bits of lumber attest to the other former village activities.

RODGERVILLE

Today's traveller speeds between the modern towns of Hensall and Exeter along a smooth paved highway. Best forgotten are those early days when Highway 4 was known as the old London Road and was a muddy quagmire which trapped luckless buggies and wagons. But, forgotten too, and regrettably so, is Rodgerville, an old village which once lined the London Road, a mile south of Hensall. Apart from a few abandoned houses and sheds straggling along the new highway,

One of Duncrief's few remaining buildings (1976).

Rodgerville is only a memory. Yet it predates both of its neighbours and at one time was the area's main town.

Although settled in 1834 by William Elder, it was not until Matthew Rodgers opened his general store and post office in 1852 that this rapidly growing farming area had its first major village. As was the contemporary custom, the post office was named after its first postmaster.

The area became prosperous and Rodgerville grew rapidly. By 1863 it boasted three general stores including that run by James Bonthron, three blacksmiths—Hislop, Porter and McLeod—Hadley Doan's tannery, Matthew Rodgers' hotel and several artisans.

Rodgerville's little frame Presbyterian church, built in 1851, served a wide area for almost half a century, under the firm guidance of Rev. John Logie. In 1886 its congregation exceeded 100 members. Rodgerville's religious residents led the temperance struggle of the last century as *The Huron Expositor* of October 14, 1870 aptly noted: "The Rodgerville Band of Hope numbers 109 members and is increasing every night. This is perhaps the largest for a country place in Canada. Much of the success of the Temperance cause is due to the zealous efforts of Rev. Logie of the Presbyterian Church."

These were Rodgerville's palmy days and few believed her destiny was anything but great. But, early in the 1870s, railway surveyors appeared. The London, Huron and Bruce Railway, it seemed, would run through Rodgerville. At first, expectations rose. However, due to the enterprise of the Petty brothers, who owned land and mills one and one-half miles north, the expected station was not built at Rodgerville but near the Petty mills. This marked the beginning of Hensall and the end of Rodgerville. Since it was more profitable for businesses to locate at a railway station, from 1876, when the railway opened, the new community of Hensall began drawing the life from old Rodgerville. One by one the businesses moved and the buildings fell vacant. Matthew Rodgers' old hotel stood empty for several years. In 1886 the congregation of the Rodgerville church chose a new site in Hensall. By

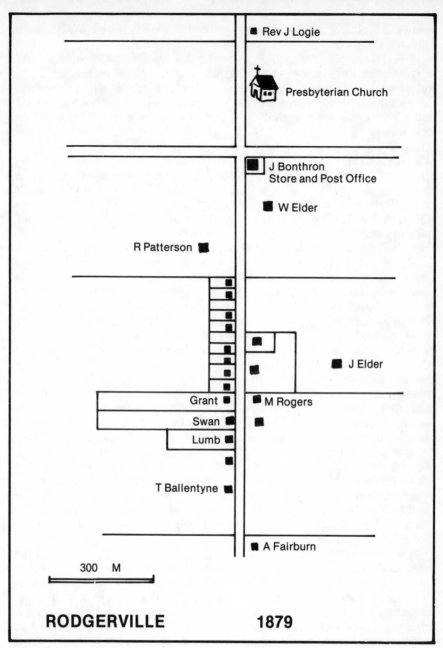

Rev J Logie

Presbyterian Church

J Bonthron
Store and Post Office

W Elder

R Patterson

J Elder

Grant

M Rogers

Swan

Lumb

T Ballentyne

A Fairburn

300   M

RODGERVILLE   1879

1890, her population a mere 45, Rodgerville contained only Bonthron's store and McLeod's blacksmith shop.

Bonthron's son, Robert, moved to Hensall and there opened a store. (The current generation of Bonthrons still operate an undertaking business in Hensall). Then, in 1899, the Rodgerville post office closed and a name which was once prominent in the area disappeared from the maps.

A former resident, Mrs. Mary Buchanan, remembers with regret the empty old church being dismantled in 1910 and moved away to an unknown fate.

A few vestiges of the old town still lie beside the new highway: original dwellings now vacant and forlorn. A couple of residences have retained their occupants over the years, but, of most of old Rodgerville, only lot lines, weedy yards and mounds of dirt where houses once stood tell of a former village that was once the focus for a busy pioneer community.

NAPIER

Although in Eastern Ontario disbanded army regiments commonly constituted the first settlers into an area—witness the settlements near Perth and Richmond—rarely was this the case in southwestern Ontario. The birth of Napier is therefore unique. In 1829 a disbanded military unit settled either side of the Sydenham Valley and, by 1838, had constructed a log school, church, and military academy.

Several years passed before the general wave of pioneer settlement swept into the area. In 1852 Colonel John Arthur and his business associate, Keefer, recognizing the excellent water power of the river and the bountiful supply of walnut timber, erected grist and sawmills. Keefer had excellent business credentials as co-founder of the earlier Keefer and Cook Company in nearby Strathroy.

A few years later the J.G. Sutherland Company moved in, acquired the flour and sawmills and built a modern woollen mill. Two lively hotels, the Napier Inn and the Sydenham House were in full swing, housing the daily influx of stage travellers from Strathroy. The list of industries grew longer and, by 1870, the little town was humming with activities which ranged from a pump factory, brickyard, and cabinet factory to shoe emporium, a wagon factory, three blacksmiths and a tinsmith. The general store, school and Wesleyan-Methodist church had been open for several years and the town acquired the services of two practising physicians, Dr. Alex Nixon and Dr. William Lindsay. Lindsay, a graduate of Victoria College, was also the coroner for Middlesex County and travelled extensively around the county. After he moved his practice to Strathroy, Dr. Nixon continued to serve the town for several years.

It was, however, John Sutherland's Napier Mills which dominated the community for several years. In an advertisement in the Strathroy *Age* of 1870, he was aiming at a wide market: "To the farmers of Middlesex: Gentlemen, good wheat, wool and saw logs are in good demand at the Napier Mills for cash or goods etc.; flour, cloths, lumber, chopped feed, bran and shorts are kept on hand...manufactured to order wholesale or retail and sold on most reasonable terms..." As if his extensive mill operations were not enough, he was also involved in real estate, for the ad continued: "Several good lots of land for sale cheap for cash or on terms."

Napier's extensive village plan comprised 120 lots on 10 streets. High Street developed into the main artery and anyone strolling down the road in 1880 would have passed Ormerod's cheese factory at the town's south end, then the wagon and blacksmith shops, the Masonic Hall and cabinet shop, all side by side, while across the road were the

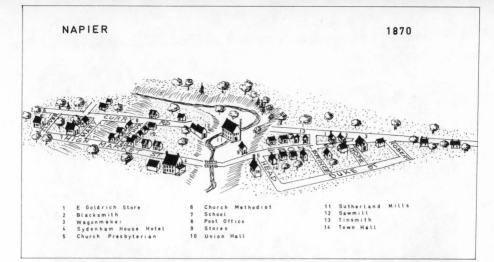

1	E Goldrich Store	6	Church Methodist	11	Sutherland Mills
2	Blacksmith	7	School	12	Sawmill
3	Wagonmaker	8	Post Office	13	Tinsmith
4	Sydenham House Hotel	9	Stores	14	Town Hall
5	Church Presbyterian	10	Union Hall		

Napier's well-hidden post office remains (1976).

tinsmith's shop, another wagon and blacksmith shop, lines of attractive homes, then the Napier Inn at the corner of Prince Street. A few yards farther on would carry the traveller to the south rim of the Sydenham River valley and the then two-year-old Presbyterian brick church, built for the "princely" sum of $1,800. From the rim he could command a magnificent view of the heart of the village, nestled in the bottom of the valley. At the foot of the hill was Calvert's general store, immediately across the river the Sydenham House, and, just upstream, the noise and clatter of John Sutherland's mills. Beyond the hotel lay the busy intersection with Arthur Street and three more stores, union hall and post office. On the opposite rim of the valley stood the brick school, the

Napier's handsome brick school (1976).

older Methodist Church and the large estate of Colonel John Arthur.

Napier at its peak was without doubt a cheerful and busy place. Township councils held their regular meetings in the Napier town hall while a variety of temperance movements organized crusades. The Strathroy *Age* of 1871 offers a glimpse of contemporary Christmas celebrations: "The first festival of Napier was held Friday evening (when) a Christmas tree was erected and adorned in the most beautiful manner by the most beautiful flowers to meet the eye... It was heavily laden with books that were to be presented to the children who attended the school... Before the hour appointed both parents and children were seen wending their way towards the church."

But Napier was to see few similar Christmases. The new railway had by-passed the village and with the same devastating blow that it dealt many country villages it robbed Napier of its market advantages. By the turn of the century the pump and cheese factories, the extensive mills of Sutherland and Company, and the many small trades were gone.

R. Dunlop continued operating his sawmill for a few years, as did Malcolm McIntosh his blacksmith shop. The general store stayed open under the capable management of A.E. Field until recent years.

Today Napier is a ghost of its former self. Here, a mile southwest of the junction of Middlesex County Roads 6 and 7, in the 7th Concession of Metcalfe township, only 5 original homes remain occupied, only 2 streets still travelled. The disused brick school and sturdy Presbyterian church stand today as splendid examples of the simple architectural beauty that marked Victorian Ontario. The once busy corner of High and Arthur Streets is now quiet and overgrown, the sagging shell of the former post office gazing vacantly from behind young trees, and the Sydenham River quietly bubbles past the sites of the old mills.

KATESVILLE

The 1830s witnessed the rise of the village of Katesville. Situated on the banks of the Sydenham River, a few miles upstream from where Napier was to grow, and two miles southwest of modern Strathroy, Katesville was a jumping-off point to Ontario's then untamed wilderness.

W.H. Smith, a geographer who travelled widely throughout the province in the 1840s and 1850s, visited the village around 1846 and described it as having a store built by Richard Brannan, and about 30 inhabitants. From this small beginning Katesville, in 11 years, grew to a thriving settlement of 150 people with 2 new stores to rival Brannan's, 2 hotels and several shops. All the buildings lined Concession 2 at the Sydenham River crossing.

The year 1846 saw something of a controversy when the two dozen residents of nearby Strathroy petitioned the government for a new post office. The area's only postmaster, R. Brown at Katesville, fearing a loss of business at his store, somehow "forgot" to forward their petition. Undaunted, Strathroy's villagers tried again at the Delaware post ofice and this time succeeded in communicating with the capital. Brown, incensed at recognition of the rival fledgling village, resigned. Fulton assumed postal duties and later passed them on to William McClatchey, Katesville's last postmaster.

In 1871 Katesville was still going strong with James Elliott's store, Sessions' smithy shop, a new hoop factory run by Matthew Wilson and Robert Whitley, as well as a carpenter, tailor and carriage maker. But this was the last year that records show Katesville as a prospering community. Strathroy had, in 1858, received a railway and Katesville's fate was sealed. After Katesville's merchants closed out or moved to Strathroy, the few remaining residents watched their village dwindle and when they left or passed away, no one replaced them.

Today the wilderness is gone, replaced by prosperous farms. Strathroy has grown from that 24 residents to 7,500. But Katesville, that once important village on the brink of Ontario's wilderness, has left nothing more than tall grasses blowing over vacant lots.

THE SOUTHWEST:

The terrain of the extreme southwestern tip of Ontario is flat, its growing season long, a combination conducive to the cultivation of a greater variety of agricultural products than is possible in other parts of Ontario. In this fertile plain comprising what are now the counties of Lambton, Kent and Essex, pioneer villages once abounded. Although most have long lost their business functions, many have, because of rural population pressures, continued as residential hamlets.

Few vanished completely, and this fact makes the stories of the following four villages unique.

SUTORVILLE

Part of the southwest in the 1850s and 1860s was considered to be a difficult if not impenetrable swamp. High water tables discouraged agricultural incursions. Valuable timber supplies tempted lumber interests but lack of easy transportation delayed exploitation until the arrival of the railways.

In anticipation of a Grand Trunk Railway extension into Brooke Township of Lambton County, William Sutor built a stave mill to tap the vast timber resources of the Brooke Swamp. There had been only one earlier mill, that built by Abraham Saunders in 1877. When the new station opened in 1892, both mills were busy shipping oak, elm and ash products. A village quickly developed at the station and within 2 years boasted a reported 75 families, a church, a school, a general store and two blacksmiths. Being but a one-industry town, it had a limited life expectancy and, indeed, in 1902 when the forests were gone, the village had served its purpose and died. Many villagers stayed in the area to farm the new lands then being created by the draining of Brooke Swamp.

For a time the station took on new life by shipping a new product, sugarbeet. By 1933 highway shipment had become cheaper than rail and the station was closed and the tracks lifted.

Thus ended Sutorville. Today, many farm houses and barns dot the flat, prairie-like horizon. However, save for an Anglican Church and a couple of old residences, no trace now remains of the stave village of Sutorville. It is impossible to perceive even the old railway alignment

OLINDA

To Ontario's early pioneers iron was almost as vital as wood. Any source of iron ore was usually seized upon with little delay. Peat bogs contained a variety of ore known as "bog ore" which, in Ontario's early days of settlement, supplied local blast furnaces throughout the province. A site 20 miles southeast of Windsor and 6 miles north of the Lake Erie shore possessed all the ingredients necessary for the production of iron: a supply of bog ore, sand, limestone and clay for mixing, and water for cooling.

Here, in the 1820s, six miles northwest of Leamington, Joseph Van Norman, famed builder of iron furnaces in other parts of southwestern Ontario, placed a new furnace and a substantial workers' village developed beside his operation.

In 1832 a local newspaper, The Canadian Emigrant and Western District Advertiser, carried this description of the activity of Olinda: "Iron of the first quality is obtained in abundance one mile from the furnace...Coal (charcoal) of which 500 bushels are used per day is made at the furnace. All other necessary materials as sand, limestone, and clay are found on the spot and from 60 to 70 men are daily employed to whom liberal wages are paid." Later accounts placed the work force at 100. The finished pig iron travelled by schooner to Toronto, Montreal and Detroit where urban growth was creating heavy demands. Although the reasons for closing are disputed, the furnace had, by the late 1840s, ceased operation. Thus Olinda, the iron town, became a ghost town.

Some years later a new "Olynda" arose. As farm settlement progressed, the needs increased for shops and trades at a convenient

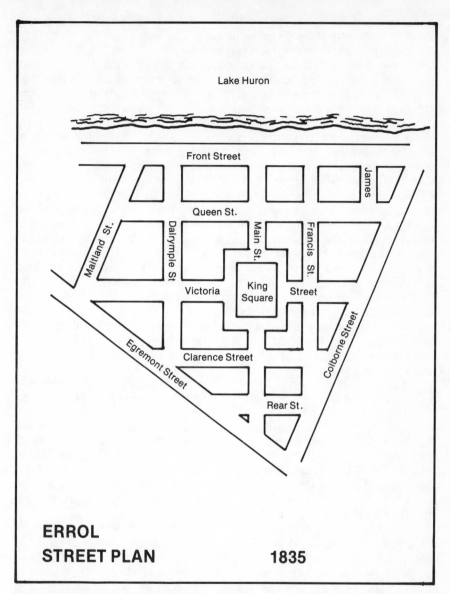

**ERROL
STREET PLAN**   **1835**

location. The vicinity of Country Road 18 and Highway 3 near the old furnace soon became the focus for pioneer businesses and took on the name "Olynda". But the old Olinda had forever vanished. Agricultural specialization became the order of the day. Fruit orchards replaced the pioneer farming and became the region's economic base. Among the orchards near the site of the old Olinda furnace and village lie rocks, slag, charcoal and the remains of an old lime kiln, the few meagre survivors of this once bustling pioneer "iron" village.

ERROL

Since the Ontario of the early 1800s was a target for American expansionism, many early settlement schemes were designed and located with a military purpose in mind and less attention was given the importance of harbour facilities or millsites.

This was, in the 1830s, the rationale for the location of Errol, near Lake Huron at the terminus of the Egremont colonization road, a site lacking harbour and water power. The village plan consisted of a nine-street grid pattern about a central square.

Although most of the town lots ended up in speculators' hands, many *bona fide* settlers arrived and Errol soon enjoyed a church, post office, two large taverns, a blacksmith, sawmill, several tradesmen, three resident magistrates and a weekly newspaper, the *Samiel*.

A few miles west, where Lake Huron's waters funnel into the St. Clair river, a rival town was growing. Port Sarnia had the advantage of a good harbour and was capturing the attention and the business of the area's settlers. Its commercial development soon began to outpace that of Errol. When the Egremont Road was extended beyond Errol to Port Sarnia, the future for Errol became bleak. The editor of the *Samiel*, George McKee, stood steadfastly by his town. In criticizing Malcum Cameron, a lumberman from Perth and proponent of Port Sarnia, McKee wrote: "The honourable gentleman, fearing that Errol should outstrip his bantling city, he commenced his career not by waging an honourable war but by a series of low, cunning, artful and delusive cajoling, takes advantage of his situation and the whole bent of his parliamentary influence is brought to bear in one grand focus like a battering ram... Malcolm succeeded, by fair or by foul means, deponent saith not, in having the London road (i.e. the Egremont Road) completed so direct communication was opened between London and Port Sarnia."

Little more than a decade later, Port Sarnia became the district's commercial and administrative capital, while Errol became a vista of forlorn buildings and overgrown streets. By 1846 the church had been removed to nearby Camlachie and soon after the sawmill closed. When the Grand Trunk Railway by-passed Errol in 1859, it dealt the final blow and Errol fell into complete decay. Yet nearly a century was to pass before, in 1940, and after much wrangling, the municipal council finally closed its streets "officially".

For many years the only symbol of old Errol had been its cemetery. But, after the Second World War, when the recreation boom spread along the Lake Huron shoreline, the area around Errol sprang back to life with swimmers, sunbathers and cottagers. Today there is little to indicate that vacant buildings and weedy streets once occupied the site.

EAST WILKESPORT

Shortly after the first settlers arrived at the north branch of the Sydenham River, 10 miles upstream from Wallaceburg, Wilkesport developed as distinct east and west villages.

The west village became the larger of the two and, in 1880, contained several stores, mills, shops, a hotel and post office, while the east village could boast of little more than a store, a steam-driven sawmill, a few artisans and several dwellings scattered along fewer than a half-dozen village streets. The pull of the larger village grew stronger and the businesses gradually moved from the east side to the west.

The east village became an abandoned relic. By 1909 only six buildings remained; by 1940, only two.

Most vestiges of the old village have long disappeared. Even the larger west village has dwindled to a smaller and quieter version of a country town that was once such a bustling business centre. Farming has remained the area's mainstay and is a vital link in Ontario's agricultural prosperity. The level countryside, now largely treeless, abounds with healthy farms. ●

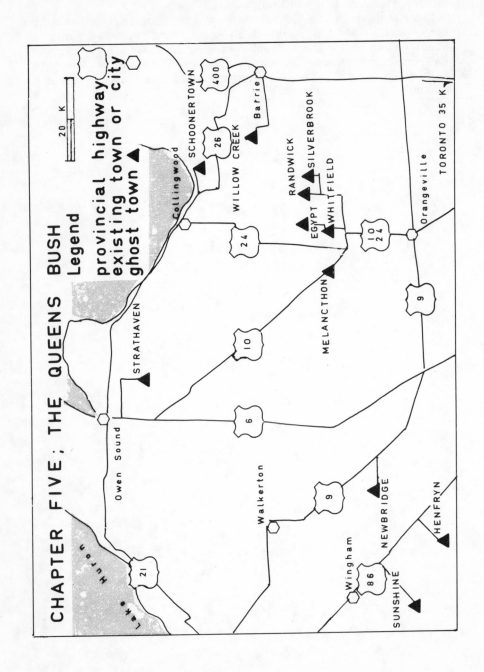

CHAPTER FIVE; THE QUEENS BUSH

Legend

provincial highway
existing town or city
ghost town ▲

20 K

Lake Huron

21

Owen Sound

STRATHAVEN ▲

Collingwood

SCHOONERTOWN ▲

400

26

WILLOW CREEK ▲

Barrie

RANDWICK ▲
SILVERBROOK ▲
WHITFIELD ▲
EGYPT ▲

24

10

6

9

Walkerton

MELANCTHON ▲

10
24

9

Orangeville

TORONTO 35 K

Wingham

86

NEWBRIDGE ▲

SUNSHINE ▲

HENFRYN ▲

5

THE QUEEN'S BUSH

By 1855 southern Ontario's farmlands were occupied. There were no new grounds to break, no new frontiers to conquer. Yet land-hungry immigrants continued to stream in and established farmers continued to seek land for their sons. Southern Ontario suddenly found itself facing a land shortage and a rural population crisis. To ease pressures the government acquired further Indian lands for settlement.

Only one tract of land large enough and near enough was the vast Indian territory known as the Queen's Bush. It lay in the northwestern part of peninsular Ontario with Georgian Bay on the north, Lake Huron on the west and the Huron Tract on the south. The area today would comprise the counties of Grey and Bruce and parts of Simcoe, Dufferin and Huron. Earlier settlement roads already connected older Georgian Bay ports with towns to the south and, once the land was surveyed, settlers began trudging northward along the crude roads. Upon arriving, they were not met by the level fertile soils and salubrious climate they had known or expected, but by steep, bouldery hills, infertile sands, limestone plains and shorter growing seasons—dismal condditions which soon disheartened even the hardiest farmers.

After peaking around 1880, the population swiftly declined. By the time of the Great Depression the Queen's Bush had lost 35,000 residents, many of whom had answered the call of the Canadian prairies which were opened in the 1880s.

101

VALLEY OF THE PINE:

Through a scenic valley cut into the Niagara Escarpment on the eastern border of the Queen's Bush, the Pine River rushes over cascades and waterfalls and out onto a flat sandy plain where it meets the Nottawasaga River and meanders quietly northward to Georgian Bay. On the sandy slopes of the Pine River there once grew strands of tall white pine, a species in great demand during Ontario's pioneer days.

It was often the practice of lumber companies to acquire licences which gave them exclusive rights to harvest timber over wide areas and within these limits erect large mills, dwellings, boarding houses, and often, stores.

At one time two company towns operated in the Pine Valley: Silverbrook and Randwick. When the pines vanished, the villages vanished, replaced in some areas, by tobacco farms, in others, by government reforestation projects. The quiet scene today is a far cry from yesterday's roar of great saws ripping into gigantic pine logs.

SILVERBROOK

One hundred and 30 years ago Silverbrook was home to 300 workers who laboured in the forests and the mills owned by the Brennan family. Although the dates of the mill operation remain obscure, accounts of the life and labours of the villagers have survived.

Most log hauling took place in winter, horse-drawn sleds being used to draw the logs from the forests to the ice of the mill pond. The spring melt would float the logs to the mill where a conveyor grasped the logs with great iron-teeth and fed them up the gangway to the saws. All waste was burned. For a time the sawn timber travelled to market via wagon until a railway spur line reached the mill and afforded a more efficient means of shipping the lumber.

Silverbrook at its peak boasted 33 houses, a store, blacksmith, large boarding house and a school, all owned by the Brennans. Most of these lined Tossorontio Concession Road 2 and the short road which led down to the mill. When a mortgage foreclosure on the school land appeared imminent, the residents of a nearby village, Tioga, schemed to stealthily remove the school building to a site in their own village. The story was retold in the Township of Tossorontio *Centennial Review*: "At one time there was apparently some rivalry between the mill communities of Tioga and Silverbrook. Tioga saw in the mortgage foreclosure an opportunity to get the school moved to a site near the present site of the Tioga Roman Catholic Church. But the Brennans were resourceful and determined to keep their school within easy reach of the children of the mill hands.

"A crew of house-movers from Hamilton was hired, their box car load of equipment shipped up to the spur line... The train arrived at four o'clock in the morning and every man at the mill was roused and ordered to be ready for work immediately.

"The moving equipment was drawn to the school site and by 9 o'clock the school was on its way down the road to the new site."

Ironically, of all Silverbrook's buildings, only the school house has remained.

One of the few remaining buildings to mark the site at Randwick (1976).

Eventually the depletion of pine forced the Brennans to close their operations and move the mill to a new licence in Muskoka. The workers moved either with the Brennans to Muskoka or to other nearby towns. Farmers then began using the denuded land for crops and pasture, although the low fertility of the sandy soils hindered these operations. More suitable uses such as reforestation and tobacco or potato farming now dominate.

Little has remained of the buildings which housed this happy lumbering community. Bushes, young trees and weed-covered mounds line the village road which connected the mill to the main concession road and the mill pond has long dried up, leaving only the outline of its former shape. Today, along Concession 2, tobacco farms abound, while, farther up the valley, in what were the Brennans' timber limits, a program of reforestation has restored the pine to the valley of that name.

RANDWICK

A short distance upstream from Silverbrook, the sawmills of Randwick ripped through the valley's great pine logs. Here the lumber company of Parkhill and Smith had established mills and a worker's village. Although the dates of mill operation are obscure, the Randwick post office opened in January, 1874. Mr. Parkhill became the first postmaster but, four years later, passed these duties on to William Henry.

The post office and school were located part-way up the valley wall at the intersection of the "sixth line" and the "25th sideroad" of Mulmur township while, in the valley bottom, a quarter of a mile to the south, were the mill, hotel and 32 workers' cottages. But Randwick was little more than a residential settlement for the mill. Other village amenities such as stores, blacksmiths, and carpenters were no closer than the crossroads village of Banda, one and a half miles north. A common site was 8 or 10 teams of horses en route up the "sixth line" to the Banda blacksmith. Parkhill's lumber cost only $5 per thousand board feet and many barns in the area today are constructed of lumber sawn at his mill.

William McClenton of nearby Black Bank recounts an experience

103

Whitfield, a sketch representing the layout of this crossroads village around 1880 (sketch by the author based on contemporary information).

told by his grandfather who bought Parkhill's lumber and often ate at Parkhill's home: "One day Mr. Parkhill told him to feed the horses and go to the house for dinner. In those days every house had a lean-to at the back door to store wood, pails, etc. In this lean-to was also the swill barrel for dish water, apple peelings, scraps, etc. to feed the pigs. This particular day the Parkhill cow had discovered that by pushing the door open she could feed on the potato peelings without an invitation. Mrs. Parkhill had put her out three or four times and just got back in the house when my grandfather opened the door. Mrs. Parkhill ran out with the broom yelling, 'You old brute, are you back again?' "

The day of the Parkhills is gone, and, as the pines vanished, so did Randwick. Along the banks of the Pine River, among the trees of the government plantation, old foundations decay while at the crossroads, a quarter-mile away, stand the former school and post office.

Hilly terrain and sandy soils drove away most of the area's early farmers. In some of the fields where horses once strained under the plough, weeds and thistles abound, and, in others, under the Ontario government's reforestation program, red and jack pines now stand in precise rows.

THE UPLANDS:

The condition of Upper Canadian roads often defied description, although many early travellers did find apt, if colourful, words to describe them. At best, the roads were cleared of stumps and boulders; at worst, they were vague trails through the dense forests. Despite such trying conditions, the Syndenham, Garafraxa and Hurontario settlement roads did open the Queen's Bush to pioneer influx.

Due to the slow rate of travel, stopping places (inns with taverns) occurred every five or six miles, the distance covered by a half-day's travel. Occasionally such places attracted other businesses and evolved into sizeable villages.

When farming was more prosperous and the roads more heavily travelled, these early villages were active. But when the Canadian West opened many farmers followed the lure of better soils and the farm population of the Queen's Bush dwindled. The concurrent trend toward urbanization wrote the final chapter for many of these old villages.

WHITFIELD

Hurontario Street was one of the first direct roads linking Port Credit on Lake Ontario and Collingwood on Georgian Bay. Provincial Highway 10 follows the original road alignment over its southernmost 30 miles and Provincial Highway 24 its northernmost 15 miles. Intermediate sections range from farm roads to rutted bush trails.

Many hotels, stopping places and villages sprang up along this important thoroughfare. Some, where the road was subsequently improved and paved, grew into important towns; others, where the road was allowed to deteriorate, were abandoned.

After pioneers settled the surrounding land and began to require shops and mills, Whitfield, an early stopping place midway along the road in Mulmur Township, Dufferin County, developed into a substantial village.

A weekly Whitfield column in the Shelburne *Economist*, a local newspaper, has left first-hand accounts of this busy village between 1870 and 1890. The warm spring days of 1884 witnessed a flurry of construction in Whitfield and the correspondent waxed optimistic over his village's future: "Our fair village is still on the road of progress. Mr.

105

Hilly Hurontario Street in Whitfield is no longer a major thoroughfare.

James Hutchison has opened out a new store for sale of jewelry and fancy goods. This will supply a long felt want and will prove very convenient for our young people in general. The boys will be able to buy their sweethearts jewelry of every description and our girls will be ornamented with all the precious gems of the east.'' Further on in the same issue: "New blacksmith shop—Mr. Fox of Primrose has opened out a blacksmith shop here for general jobbing.''

A week later, the *Economist* reported: "Mr. J. Greenwood just completed a new sawmill and is preparing to saw any quantity of logs.'' More businesses were needed, and wanted: "We want a shoemaker, a harnessmaker, a barber, and last but not least, a branch of the Lord's army.''

Later in that year the Orangemen of Whitfield set about constructing the area's first Orange Lodge. "The Orangemen of this place are making preparations for the erection of a hall...would advise they make it a good size as it will enable them to rent it for different purposes... such a hall is greatly needed. The site is a convenient one on the corner nearly opposite the English Church''.

The 1880s and '90s saw the clustering about the crossroads of three stores, three blacksmiths, two sawmills, and a lime kiln, as well as three churches, a school, the Orange Lodge and about a hundred residents. Daily stages connected Whitfield with Shelburne and Primrose at a cost of 25 cents for a one-way ride.

Whitfield's steadiest resident businessman was Parsons D. Henry. American-born, he and his parents had migrated from the United States to Prescott in eastern Ontario. He later moved to the busy new mill town of Hornings Mills, a few miles west of the future site of Whitfield. Henry settled on a farm near Hurontario Street where he taught school for several years before building one of Whitfield's first general stores. Then, in 1908, after moving to the nearby village of Melancthon Station, Parsons Henry died.

The route which the surveyors had selected for Hurontario Street proved a headache for travellers. Steep hills, deep swamps, and sheer cliffs made its central portions impassable and wise travellers selected alternate routes. One which became particularly popular was a north-south concession road one mile to the west. As communities along this better road grew more accessible and more popular, Whitfield, and other communities on Hurontario Street, found themselves in a backwater. Gradually the shops closed and the villages dwindled.

The departure of Parsons Henry seemed to signal the beginning of the end for Whitfield for, in the years that followed, Whitfield's shops and industries fell silent.

The central section of Hurontario Street has since become a local farmers' road while the alternative route to the west has become the busy Provincial Highway 10. Once-busy villages are only memories and little remains of their homes and shops. But time has left some vestiges of Whitfield. At the intersection today are two churches, a few vacant buildings, and several overgrown yards. Other parts of the village site have been ploughed up and crops now grow, or cattle graze, where the busy shops once stood.

EGYPT

Egypt, a lumber village on Hurontario Street, appeared and disappeared almost as suddenly. On February 28, 1885, the following article appeared in the Shelburne *Economist* "Egypt. Your many readers will be surprised to hear tell of such a place but it lies a few lots to the north of Whitfield. It presents a romantic appearance not only for its hills and dales but also for its beautiful river. It has a sawmill and large lumber trade...also a weekly mail every Saturday and a new school with an enrollment of 38."

One of the many doomed places on old Hurontario Street, Egypt survived only a few years, the *Economist* soon terming it "a remote part of our township".

Today the road to Egypt is scarcely passable, and the post office lies in ruins. While the sawmill and its workers are gone, the dam and mill pond are yet evident. The Pine River valley is one of exceptional beauty and is a popular haunt for Sunday drivers, photographers and hikers.

MELANCTHON STATION

Usually, where the railway led, prosperity followed. As the story of Melancthon Station illustrates, this was not always the case.

The Garafraxa settlement road from Shelburne to Owen Sound had been built to entice settlers into the unbroken lands of the Queen's Bush. Along its length several hotels, taverns and stopping places appeared, including two operated by Beachell and O'Boyle, near what was called the "Melancthon Corners," a major road intersection in the middle of Melancthon Township, in what was then a part of Grey County (and now forms part of Dufferin County). In 1870 J.W. Morey opened the first store and hotel at the corner itself, and Melancthon was born.

The advent of Toronto, Grey, Bruce Railway line in the 1870s stimulated the production and shipment of grain and logs. In 1877, on the lot

Melancthon Station, a sketch representing the appearance of this busy station village around 1880 (sketch by the author based upon contemporary information).

A sign on a building is the sole modern indication of this once busy village. (1975).

adjacent to the station at Melancthon, James Sloane built a steam-driven sawmill to produce logs, poles and shingles. James McCue later constructed a grain elevator, subsequently acquired by the Canada Grain Company of Toronto.

The town, renamed Melancthon Station, became the area's social and administrative capital. The town hall witnessed routine township council meetings and fiery political oratory. The Methodist Church welcomed proponents of the temperance movement while the Loyal Orange Lodge provided an outlet for Ulstermen. A public school opened just in time for the start of the 1886 fall term.

According to the *Economist* for 1890: "A stranger crossing from Melancthon Station...would imagine himself entering the suburbs of a city."

On June 2, 1886, fire almost consumed the village. The *Economist* reported: "Yesterday as hands in the sawmill had shut down for the dinner hour...smoke was seen issuing from the mill and at once surmising that the building was on fire all hands turned out and an alarm was raised. It was useless to save the mill and attention was turned to saving surrounding property." Although the town was saved, the loss of the mill dealt the town a severe blow: "The burning of the mill is quite a loss to the neighbourhood for upon it the bread and butter of quite a few depend. Remove the mill from here and the town would sink into oblivion". (Shelburne *Economist*, June 3, 1886).

Within three months Sloane had replaced the mill with one newer and bigger, and its tall chimney soon became a local landmark. It operated steadily until 1912. The 1880s and '90s were the peak years for Melancthon Station "...with a busy general store, a first class hotel, the familiar ring of the blacksmith's anvil and the shrill sound of the sawmill's whistle...Melancthon was a veritable hive of industry." There were, in addition, the station, the school, church, Orange Lodge, grain elevator, a carpenter, cooper, contractor, and a population of 200.

Although, after Sloane died, no one wished to continue the sawmill in light of dwindling timber supplies, Melancthon's decline was not sudden. Mike Callaghan, the blacksmith, carried on for several years as did the church and school. The grain elevator operated into the '20s. The general store never closed and thus presents an anomaly in our ghost town annals. It operates to this day with gas pumps, a restaurant and a bold sign declaring "Melancthon." Although the old town hall and school still stand, the other buildings have gone, and the once busy station area is now just an overgrown field.

As for the other buildings—the old shops, the mills, the elevator, and the many homes—only weeds grow amid foundations and along the old village lot lines.

STRATHAVEN

Over tens of thousands of years the Beaver and Bighead Rivers steadily carved their now spectacular valleys into the limestone layers of the Niagara Escarpment. Their rushing waters ensured many power sites for the early mills of pioneer Ontario, including the saw and grist mills which became the basis for a busy village on the eighth concession of Holland Township, Grey County.

Strathaven's buildings developed along McNab Avenue, a side street linking the 8th concession road with the mills, a quarter of a mile away. Leading off McNab Avenue were two short cul-de-sacs and a river road where a few shops and residences also sprang up.

Through Strathaven's formative years J. Thomas and Son operated flour, saw and shingle mills which attracted other shops and trades. After a few years, McNab Avenue boasted two general stores (those of Joseph Long and W.J. McKessock), a blacksmith, wagon maker, school, Baptist Church and Forresters Hall. McKessock's store, in a 1904 advertisement, offered a wide variety of goods, including "fur coats, caps, gauntlets, imitation fur caps, kid gloves, horse blankets, whips (and) mocassins," and claimed to be "headquarters for fancy China and Christmas toys. Don't fail to see them." For bartering and purchasing, McKessocks issued their own wooden "coins."

A new church, finished in 1900, replaced an old frame building which, for the nominal sum of $40, was given to the Forresters as a

109

Looking west along Strathaven's McNab Avenue circa 1900.

Strathaven's McNab Ave., once bustling, now ends quietly in a field beside one of the few remaining buildings (1976).

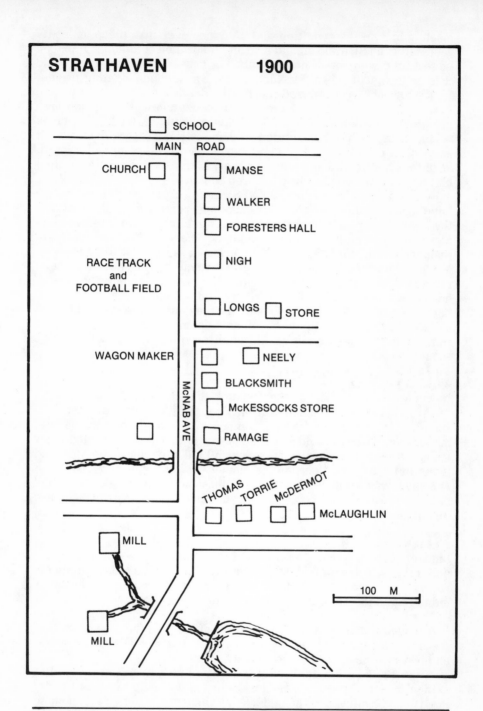

STRATHAVEN **1900**

SCHOOL

MAIN ROAD

CHURCH

MANSE

WALKER

FORESTERS HALL

NIGH

RACE TRACK
and
FOOTBALL FIELD

LONGS STORE

WAGON MAKER

NEELY

BLACKSMITH

McKESSOCKS STORE

McNAB AVE

RAMAGE

THOMAS TORRIE McDERMOT

McLAUGHLIN

MILL

100 M

MILL

Several of Strahaven's residents in 1916 beside McKessock's store.
Front Row: Lou Mustard, Bill Laird, Will McKessock, Jim Morrison; Back Row:
Ernie McKibbon, Ed Howey, Cecil Sparrow, Mancel Hewitt, Tom McCarthur,
Carson McKessock.

meeting hall on the condition that no dance ever take place under its roof. Although Strathaven had a strict intolerance of dancing, it placed no restrictions on horse racing, football or baseball. The large track and field on the north side of McNab Avenue was a popular gathering spot for the township's racing and sports afficionados.

With the close of the 19th century, urbanization was well underway in Ontario. Owen Sound, just 20 miles west, and Meaford, a few miles north, became the area's retail and industrial centres. Along with many country villages, Strathaven began its decline. The mills closed, as did the blacksmith and wagon maker. About 1917, Long demolished his store and moved his house to Owen Sound.

By the depression of the 1930s, Strathaven had shrunk to just 10 buildings, including the church, school and Forresters hall. Following the war, more of Strathaven came tumbling down until, today, Strathaven virtually exists in name only. The school is now a private residence, the millsites are long disused, and only a house and McCessock's former store remain. The two cul-de-sacs have long been reclaimed by fields of grain, as have the race track and the row of homes which parallelled the river. Only foundations tell of the Forresters hall and a rusting baseball cage denotes the sports field. In spite of the surrounding scene of abandonment, the Baptist Church remains to this day an active and vital focus for the residents of this scenic North Grey farming area.

HURON SLOPES:

In the western portion of the Queen's Bush, the land slopes gently toward the shores of Lake Huron. Deep fertile soils attracted and sustained a prosperous farming community. Through the area several meandering rivers provided water power sites which attracted early mills. Several villages sprang up around millsites along the Maitland River but, with the decrease in timber and the superior rivalry of railway towns, many fell into ruin. While some struggled along as small clusters of retirement homes, Henfryn, Sunshine and Newbridge have all but disappeared.

HENFRYN

Industry thrives yet at Henfryn. On the banks of the Maitland, fine, pure clays which supplied the village's first brickyard today supply the kilns of Henfryn's tile factory. However, little remains of the other industries and businesses which formed the Henfryn of the last century.

Although time has obscured the birth of the village, it is known that there was an early mill on the river. The growth of a village, however, had to await the arrival of the railway.

In the 1870s, after the Wellington, Grey and Bruce Railway built a station in Grey Township, Huron County, a half-mile north of County Road 6, and 3 miles west of modern-day Highway 23, a number of small industries and businesses gathered and Henfryn blossomed into a thriving village. The Huron County Atlas for 1878 has left this contemporary description: "Henfryn and Ethel (a nearby village) are railroad villages... The former (Henfryn) is much the more important of

112

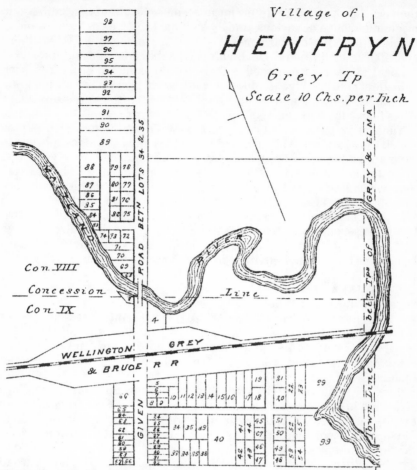

Town plan of the village of Henfryn circa 1879 (from the ILLUSTRATED HISTORICAL ATLAS OF THE COUNTY OF HURON).

The quiet railway crossing which was once the flourishing village of Henfryn.

the two, however, containing large steam mills, taverns, stores and mechanics shops of various kinds." William King was proprietor of the hotel, W.L. Wills of the general store; C. Heible and J.D. Williams operated sawmills and E. Davis shipped lumber from the station.

Local clays proved excellent for brick-making and Henfryn soon gained fame for its high quality brickyards which supplied a wide area. Mittleholz, Selwood and Jacob Hanofer operated the yards at various times between 1880 and 1900.

The heady optimism of the 1800s saw an ambitious town survey which gave Henfryn 98 lots. But, despite the railway, the town began to stagnate and most of the village lots remained unsold. As rival towns attracted new industries, Henfryn declined and, one by one, the hotel, the church, the Grand Trunk station, the mills and the general store closed, although George Michael did continue to operate the store well into the 1930s. Of the old houses, only two remain occupied, the rest being represented by foundations and overgrown lots. Even though new owners of two of the old village lots are constructing modern homes, the bustle and activity of former days will never be repeated.

SUNSHINE

Sunshine, at first, was but a mill powered by the Maitland River where the 10th sideroad of Morris Township, Huron County, crossed it. After a few years, other pioneer businesses located there and, by 1890, Sunshine's business included, in addition to the saw and grist mills, Isaac Rogerson's chair factory, Robert Crittenden's general store and Richard Webb's blacksmith shop.

George Michie of nearby Wingham recalls how Sunshine's buildings stretched in a single line along the east side of the road from the river to the junction, with modern County Road 16 a few hundred yards to the north. A boardwalk ran past the businesses and the dwellings. At the junction, and kitty-corner to the shops, a church and a small adjacent cemetery were situated. But Sunshine was ignored by the railroad and became a backwater. Gradually her businesses folded and residents moved away, leaving only a few mounds in the fields and pastures. Now only the cemetery is to be seen—an ironic monument to a dead village.

NEWBRIDGE

As settlement crept further into the forests of the Maitland River watershed, Newbridge, in Howick Township, Huron County, six miles west of modern day Listowel, burst into local prominence as another of those "water power" villages with promises of future greatness. If her initial rapid growth is an indicator, Newbridge indeed appeared destined to be a village of some importance. But those golden days have long since passed and only a few old buildings, some vacant, some still occupied, remain.

Initially a site for pioneer saw and grist mills, Newbridge, or Spencetown as it was first known, covered a considerable range of pioneer activities by 1872. In addition to the saw and grist mills owned by Charles Ferrand and operated by Robert Elliot, there were two hotels, a blacksmith, and a general store with post office operated by

Newbridge's store and Main Street in busier times.

James Carson, as well as such trades as shoemaker, harness maker, carpenter and weaver. A village plot included 30 lots along Concession Four and the side street leading to the mill.

The closing decades of the last century saw the village prosper, its population rising from 130 in 1872, to 200 in 1884, along with the establishing of new mills and places of business. A stagecoach operated daily between Newbridge and the nearby village of Fordwich.

One by one the mills closed and the tradesmen moved to the more profitable railway boom towns. The dawn of the 20th century saw only 4 industries remaining and a population reduced by half. In spite of the village's decline, J.W. Spence operated his sawmill for a number of years as did R. Bowes the general store, while the doors to Adam Pinn's hot and noisy smithy shop remained open.

Thirty years later, only nine buildings remained along the street, while the road to the mill had become an almost forgotten trail.

The Newbridge of today is unidentifiable as a village—only the Methodist Church and a couple of houses remain. Quiet has settled over the millsite and the Maitland River rushes, unimpeded, towards Lake Huron.

THE WILLOW CREEK CONTROVERSY

High on a bluff guarding the lush green stillness of the Minesing Swamp, on the eastern perimeter of the Queen's Bush, Ontario's most controversial ghost town is again rising from its overgrown grave amid sporadic but energetic controversy.

Was there ever a village of "Willow Creek?" Although the existence of the military depot is not in question, local historians support the existence of a sizeable village at Willow Creek, while Ontario government historians poo-poo the existence of any village and downplay the size of the fort itself.

Both sides do agree on the events leading up to the selection of the site for a military depot.

In those days, when war raged off and on between the Canadian colonies and the new United States, safe transportation of troops and military supplies was paramount. Strategists seeking to avoid the American warships lurking in the Great Lakes chose an overland route via Yonge Street, Lake Simcoe and the Nottawasaga River to Georgian Bay, where supplies could safely be shipped to the vital upper lakes garrisons.

Depots were established at four points along this route: at what is now the village of Holland Landing, at the foot of an old Indian trail known as the nine-mile portage (it grew to be the town of Barrie), at Willow Creek, the terminus of the portage, and at the mouth of the Nottawasaga River, near the present village of Wasaga Beach. The Willow Creek depot, high on a sandy bluff, commanded a magnificent and strategic view of the swamp below and the landing on Willow Creek, one-quarter mile distant. Previously, the portage had been used by the voyageurs of the North West Company, who had built a storehouse and clerk's residence at the site. During the War of 1812, the British erected a blockhouse, a stockade, and several living quarters on the bluff, and warehouses at the landing.

Willow Creek Depot played an active and vital role in Upper Canada's military defense strategy. Small barges, or "batteaux," twisted 'neath overhanging willows along the meandering creek with supplies for the Nottawasaga estuary settlement of Schoonertown and the Drummond Island garrison far across Georgian Bay.

During the hostilities of 1812-14, and for a few years after, along this military transportation route flowed flour, pork, salt, shoes and candles, all destined for the upper lakes. But the popularity of the route declined when the end of the war re-opened the all-water great lakes route. As reported by Sir George Head in 1815, the nine-mile-long portage had fallen into a poor state of repair "...being merely a track where the trees had been partially felled by the axe, and the stumps even of these very imperfectly removed."

Of the depot at Willow Creek, we have this contemporary description: "...Here were several log houses scarcely habitable—but much better than the dwellings at Kempenfeldt which the men took possession of and the mid and myself took up our quarters in a small room adjoining the house of Commisarys Clerk in charge of the stores; the frost settling in anew, I expect to be detained here some time, and

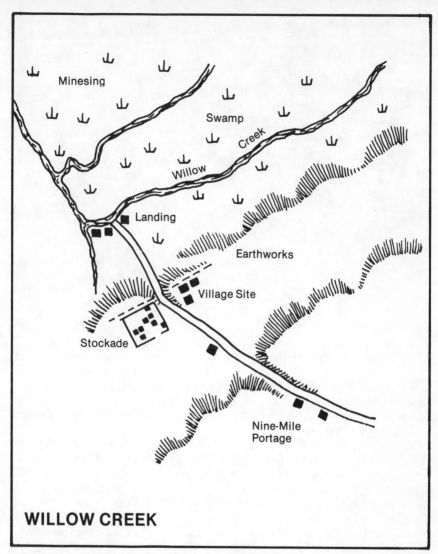

WILLOW CREEK

the men having no employment I set them to work to build me a house with logs, after the fashion of the country, which occupied them till the 29th, and when finished, I took possession, but it was like the house I somewhere read of 'In fine weather it admitted no wet and when it rained the water was not prevented from running out.' "

There were also a cook-house, stable and a blockhouse. Two older temporary log storehouses had fallen into disrepair and were replaced by a larger building, some 60'x20' of flattened timber and shingles. Three large storehouses on stilts stood in the swamp by the landing until destroyed by the heavy flood of 1819. Inducements to pioneer settlers along the nine-mile portage were partially successful and several log houses appeared along the road. One of these was a tavern operated by a man named "Playter" or "Playtoff". The settlement remained quite busy until 1830 or so, when traffic began using the

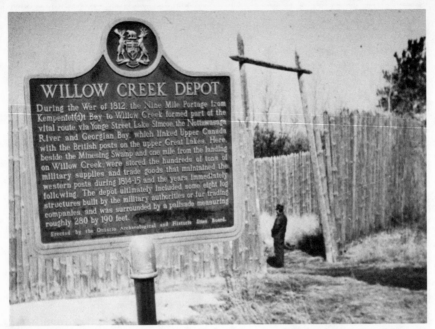

An attempt by provincial authorities to reconstruct the old Willow Creek Depot has faltered somewhat and vandalism has set in—this placque was a victim.

newly opened and more direct Penetanguishene Road, which linked Lake Simcoe directly with Georgian Bay at Penetanguishene, the site of a new military garrison. By 1835 the depot and its storehouses were reported to be in disrepair.

The size and even the existence of a village at Willow Creek Depot is vigorously disputed. Simcoe County historian Andrew Hunter claims there indeed was a village at that location. In 1948 he wrote, "In consequence of the great amount of traffic quite a little village arose at the northwestern terminus of the portage on Willow Creek. The late Thomas Drury Sr. was married at this village in its palmy days and the place otherwise manifested the usual signs of social life."

Robert Thom, an expert in the Georgian Bay area, felt the hamlet began in 1818, reached its peak in the 1820s, and declined around 1830. He indicates that CPR builders unearthed unidentified graves at the site.

Disputing the existence of the hamlet, a report by the Ontario Ministry of Culture and Recreation hypothesizes that, since early travellers over the Portage failed to mention a village, therefore none existed. The report also suggests that since the road was often in poor repair, no one would settle along it.

Yet an archaeological survey of Wilfrid and Elsie Jury, of the University of Western Ontario, has unearthed foundations of several log buildings beside the old route which date from the time the route experienced its heaviest use. It is logical, therefore, to conclude that, since non-military settlement probably existed along the road, there would have been a non-military settlement at the depot itself. A

118

"hamlet" of early upper Canada was seldom more than a small collection of residences, and seldom of a size to warrant a travellers' notation.

As the use of the portage dwindled, the settlers moved away to other parts of the township then being surveyed, leaving "Willow Creek" to the winds and the weeds. Hamlet or not, the portage, the depot and all buildings were abandoned by 1835 and Willow Creek became one of southern Ontario's earliest ghost towns.

The historian, Hunter, visited the site in 1948 and found little more than "the outlines of the foundations of a few buildings, covering in all about a quarter of an acre." In 1956 the Jury expedition measured six cellars at the fort and two foundations along the road near the fort. Along the portage trail they investigated foundations of log buildings, wild apple trees and wagon ruts.

Today's visitor, however, finds a new "Willow Creek" rising from the earth. The Nottawasaga Valley Conservation Authority has partially reconstructed the old depot and the Ontario government has erected an historic plaque. From the wooden palisade where the blockhouse once stood, the visitor can gaze across the same untouched swamp as did the troops and the traders of 1820.

Beside the fort he can almost hear the clank and rattle of the wagons as they descended the bluff into the swamp and approached the Landing. On either side of the old roadway, among the young trees and underbrush, the visitor can still discern the earthenworks and, perhaps, discover an old squared nail, a piece of a broken rum bottle, or a pioneer axe head.

SCHOONERTOWN

Ironically the War of 1812 was over when the building of Fort Nottawasaga or Schoonertown was commissioned. News travelled slowly, however, and when Commodore Sir Edward Owen learned that hostilities had ceased, he decided that, since the plans for Schoonertown were so advanced, and that since renewed war activities were likely, construction should proceed.

The choice of the site, four miles from the mouth of the Nottawasaga River, had been his. A fast supply route to the strategic garrison at Michillimackinac (near modern Sault Ste. Marie) was imperative. The Nottawasaga River route was the fastest and Owen therefore selected the river mouth, which had already been developed, as the site for a naval establishment. For a time a blockhouse stood nearby and it was there that American warships sank the British schooner Nancy in one of the more famous incidents of the war.

In the winter of 1814-15 the crews of the schooners Surprise and Confiance had erected winter quarters. By the summer of 1815, these buildings had been burned and new ones were ordered. When finished, Schoonertown boasted some eleven buildings including a captain's quarters, two officers' sleeping quarters, an officers' mess, two barracks, a seamen's mess, purser's store room, one or two blacksmiths, a technician's building, and, unofficially, one house of prostitution. The latter was run by Mrs. Asher Mundy who, during the war, had operated such an enterprise in Hogg's Hollow near Toronto.

But with the erection of Schoonertown she had moved her establishment.

From the beginning Owen intended that Schoonertown would be only temporary, as a permanent garrison was being planned for Penetanguishene, a site several miles to the east. Poor harbour protection and a shifting sandbar made Schoonertown too inconvenient for a permanent base, whereas the sheltered waters of Penetanguishene Harbour were ideal. In 1817 the Penetang' garrison was ready and the entire naval establishment—including that of Mrs. Mundy—vacated the rivermouth. The site was quickly reclaimed by nature and, by 1833, only Mrs. Mundy's empty log building remained.

During this century the mouth of the Nottawasaga River, renamed Wasaga Beach, has become a haven for summer holidayers. Hundreds of tiny cottages have sprung up, cheek by jowl, and crowds jam the long sweeping beach. The Schoonertown site was quickly built over. Recent revitalization of interest in the Nottawasaga route has led to some excavations and a number of reports on the garrison. But, to date, the only vestige of that period is the museum built near the site where the *Nancy* went down. ●

6

ROADS OF BROKEN DREAMS

Southern Ontario's terrain is distinctly divided between the rocky Canadian Shield of the north and the fertile pleistocene plains of the south.

By 1850 the fertile southern plains had reached crowded proportions and the government of Ontario was forced to look to settling the Shield. Until this time, the steep rock outcroppings and vast, swampy intervals even spurned travel, much less permanent settlements. But, deluded by overly-optimistic reports of early surveyors, authorities believed that the soils of that portion of the Shield between the Ottawa River and Georgian Bay, known as the "Ottawa Huron Tract," held great potential for agriculture. Surely soil that grew trees must grow crops! Undaunted, the government, in 1853, launched a massive scheme to open the Tract for settlement.

Beginning with the Opeongo Road, the Hastings Road and the Addington Road, the government went on to initiate more than 20 colonization road schemes in a 12-year period. To lure prospective settlers, the government provided the incentive of free land along the roads. Each settler would receive free title to 100 acres if he, in four years, cleared 12 acres, erected a house 18'x20' and maintained his share of the road. In 1868 the free grants were extended to cover the entire Tract and the lot size doubled to 200 acres.

Initial settlement seemed to justify the effort. Many lots were taken, initial crops were good, and the lumber camps provided a market for the products. Busy villages popped up at millsites, crossroads and transfer points. But, after a few years, the scheme turned sour. The soils, after producing initial bumper crops, proved to be infertile, the

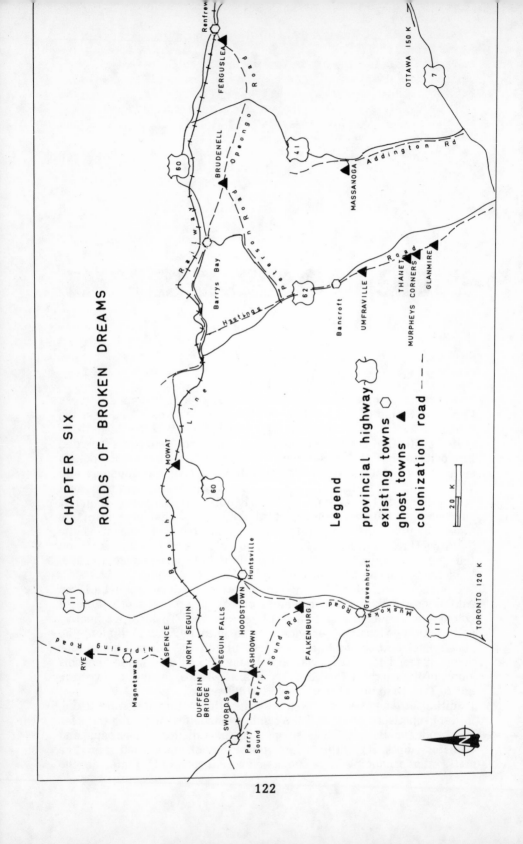

CHAPTER SIX

ROADS OF BROKEN DREAMS

Legend

provincial highway

existing towns

ghost towns

colonization road

20 K

OTTAWA 150 K

TORONTO 120 K

Renfrew

FERGUSLEA

BRUDENELL

Opeongo Road

Peterson Road

Railway

Barrys Bay

Hastings

MASSANOGA

Addington Rd

41

62

Bancroft

UMFRAVILLE

THANET Road

MURPHEYS CORNERS

GLANMIRE

60

MOWAT

Booth Line

60

Huntsville

SPENCE

NORTH SEGUIN

SEGUIN FALLS

HOODSTOWN

ASHDOWN

FALKENBURG

Parry Sound Rd

Muskoka Road

Gravenhurst

69

SWORDS

Parry Sound

DUFFERIN BRIDGE

Nipissing Road

RYE

Magnetawan

11

11

N

growing season too short. Annual forest fires burned away much of the fertile humus which had covered the bedrock. The supposedly reliable market for sale of farm products—the lumber camp operators—soon ignored local farmers and imported cheaper products from the south. Finally, in the 1880s, the Canadian West was opened and beckoned the disheartened farmers to the stone-and-stump-free fertile prairie lands. Widespread depopulation followed and long stretches of the colonization roads were abandoned in a short span of time.

Of the numerous villages which had appeared on the map, only a very few achieved sizeable proportions. Most failed to grow beyond hamlet status; and of those that did many declined or disappeared. Portions of the colonization roads have been absorbed into the provincial highway system and now rush cottagers to the attractive lakes which abound in the Shield. Thus some areas of the Ottawa-Huron Tract are enjoying an economic revitalization, and the old roads are coming back to life with gas stations and fast food outlets. But, in other areas, beyond the noise of the traffic, the old roads are reverting to forest, their old farm buildings tumbling down, and the one-time villages forlornly reflecting on dreams that turned to despair.

THE MUSKOKA ROAD:

More familiar to Muskoka's modern cottagers as the frequently clogged Highway 11, the Muskoka Road was begun nearly 120 years ago, in 1858. By the mid-1860s it had reached Huntsville and, by the 70s, Sundridge.

Its condition was much criticized. In 1863 J.W. Bridgeland, in his annual report on the condition of colonization roads, lamented: "A road that was never tolerably good has relapsed from a creditable condition to its present almost impassable one by neglect of good keeping." And in an 1871 letter, a more spirited observation by the newly arrived Mrs. Harriet King, as quoted in Letters From Muskoka (Muskoka and Haliburton): "Oh! the horrors of that journey. The road was most dreadful! Our first acquaintance with 'corduroy roads'— your poor sister had to cling convulsively to the rope to avoid being thrown out and for long afterward we both suffered from the bruises."

Nevertheless, pioneer settlers from the over-crowded south, lured by the free grants, poured into the area. Several hotels, stopping places, millsites and trans-shipment points developed into villages. Only three, Huntsville, Bracebridge, and Gravenhurst, ever attained any size of consequence. The rest stagnated or dwindled altogether.

FALKENBURG

Deep in Muskoka, at a forgotten junction on the old Muskoka Road, lie the ghosts of Falkenburg. Here, where the government in 1862 opened the Parry Sound Road to link the Muskoka Road with Georgian Bay, Falkenburg sprang up.

North and south of the "Y" intersection, 50 lots were created along the Muskoka Road and soon sprouted dwellings and businesses. Falkenburg gave every indication of becoming a thriving village and was described by contemporaries as having the greatest potential of all fledgling villages in that part of Muskoka.

Falkenburg Methodist Church, built in 1870s.

In 1882 it contained two hotels, an Anglican church, blacksmith shop, saw and shingle mills belonging to Matthias Moore, and had a daily stage service to Bracebridge and Parry Sound. Stephen Fish and Charles Sevear operated the hotels, Ed and William Hay and Hila Amont the stores, while J. Roscoe was for years the village smithy.

Then a series of changes in the transportation network combined to doom this upstart. The first was the railway which had edged north from Bracebridge and established a station a mile to the south of the road junction. Here, developed the new village of "Falkenburg Station" and the importance of the old junction diminished. Another blow was dealt by the diversion of the Muskoka Road to follow the railway tracks. Old Falkenburg became a backwater.

The final blow came during the present century when Highway 11 was built several miles to the east to handle increasing north-south traffic. Eventually the Parry Sound-Muskoka Road junction deteriorated to a dead-end road which passes through a regenerating forest near what is now Highway 532, four miles north of Bracebridge. Of the old village, a couple of original houses are still occupied, others lie abandoned. A newer sawmill, erected a few lots from Moore's original mill, has also fallen into disuse. Only a cemetery has survived to show where the church once stood, while a new house occupies the original hotel site at the junction.

The stillness of this once-busy location is now broken only by the whistles of trains speeding along the busy CNR line.

HOODSTOWN

During Muskoka's heady days of free-lot settlement, land speculation struck the north shore of Lake Vernon. Here, just four miles west of the Muskoka Road and the town of Huntsville, landowners, in optimistic

 Now demolished, these shells were part of the once promising village of Falkenburg (Photo, the author, 1967).

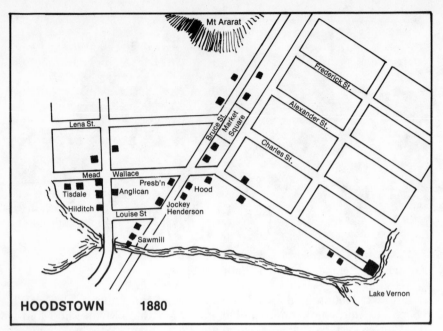

HOODSTOWN   1880

anticipation of obtaining a station on the Toronto and North Bay Railway, subdivided their early free grant farm lots into an extensive town plan, the thriving but short-lived village of Hoodstown.

By 1877 a post office named "Lake Vernon" was opened and, on a nearby set of rapids that cascaded into the tranquil lake, Charles Hood erected a sawmill. The railway construction crews were then on the horizon, moving inexorably northward. Between the rapids and a rocky granite hill known as Mt. Ararat, Janet Hood registered a plan of sub-division and sold, in a short space of time, 111 lots—most to absentee speculators who envisioned that the advent of the railway would drive up land values. All told, Hoodstown included 276 lots on 9 streets. Although most lots remained empty, many did spawn village enterprises.

On Hewson Street, the main road between the bridge and Mt. Ararat, were three general stores run by Richard Meade, Ed Hilditch and a Mr. Tisdale respectively. Opposite Tisdale's store stood the Anglican Church and, on Wallace Street, the Presbyterian Church. A third church of unremembered denomination occupied the corner of Hoodstown Road and Wallace Street. By the rapids hummed Hood's sawmill. Scattered along the remaining streets were a dozen or so residences. Hoodstown's link to Huntsville, at the foot of the lake, was the popular old sidewheeler, the *Northern*.

At the corner of Bruce and Wallace Streets stood "Jockey" Henderson's notorious hotel. As remembered by early resident W.H. Demaine, "Jockey was short, fairly stout and bald, and of Scottish ancestry. His best business occurred when the lumbermen were taking a log drive through the town. There were some things about these rivermen that Jockey resented. For instance a number of them would enter the bar, pick Jockey up and toss him like a ball to his comrade

126

who in turn passed him onto another and so on while others of the crowd helped themselves to the liquor. At the end of one of these fracasses Jockey was so annoyed that he threatened them with the law. After much haranguing the foreman of the drive managed to mollify Jockey and to make a settlement.''

Hoodstown's palmy days were short-lived. In 1886 the advancing railway line took an unexpected bend to the east and passed through Huntsville rather than Hoodstown. Dreams disintegrated. By 1891 the post office had closed; by the turn of the century the lots were once again vacant. Of these the forest has reclaimed most. Although Bruce Street still twists along Lake Vernon's shores to Huntsville, and what was once Hewson Street crosses the Hoodstown bridge, the village is little more than a memory—one that, as the oldtimers pass away—is fast fading. Toronto's cottagers now race high-speed motorboats over Lake Vernon's waters, oblivious to the fact that, in more placid days, there stood on her shores a town with visions of greatness.

THE HASTINGS ROAD:

Even though they were described as "capable both as to soil and climate of producing abundant crops of winter wheat and crops of every description,'' the lands through which much of the Hastings Road passed were scarcely amenable to being surveyed, much less being tilled. Nevertheless, construction began in 1854 and, by 1863, 1,031 settlers had moved to their free grant lots. However, no settlers arrived in 1863. Then, one by one, farms were abandoned as many farmers fled to Western Canada where, they hoped, they would never again face fields of stones and hard granite outcrops as those which had confronted them on the Hastings Road. Between 1855 and 1925, of over 400 farm lots granted, only 75 remained occupied.

St. Margaret's Church, Glanmire, in recent years before demolition.

The old church steps now lead to nothing. Glanmire, 1977.

Those who remained vainly endeavoured to market their produce in the lumber camps and to supplement their meagre incomes through the sale of potash, a product derived from the ash of burnt wood.

Many of the stopping places and millsites which had struggled to attain hamlet size stagnated, dwindled and died.

In 1925 Ontario land surveyor C.F. Aylesworth sadly reflected upon the current state of Ontario's longest colonization road: "...The mute evidence of it all is empty, dilapidated and abandoned houses and barns, orchards, wells, old broken down wooden fences, root cellars, and many other similar evidences of having given up the ghost. When first settled, there were many hotels and stopping places along this road, perhaps at intervals of every five or six miles. In many cases now it is only the old timer who can point out where they stood, so completely has all evidence of their position been obliterated."

Provincial Highway 62 follows much of the old road at its northern and southern ends. In the barren central section, however, some 14 miles are now impassible. Here the abandonment was virtually complete; here lie the ghost towns of the Hastings Road. Between Millbridge and Bancroft, where the Hastings Road varies between dirt road and bush track, lie the old villages of Glanmire, Murphy Corners, Thanet, Ormsby and Umfraville.

GLANMIRE

Six miles north of Millbridge, at a towering 60-foot-high concrete bridge spanning the turbulent Beaver Creek, the passable portion of the Hastings Road now ends. But in the days when the road was the area's major highway, a busy little village stood only a few hundred yards north of the bridge.

Murphy Corners, with two old pioneer homes, including that of its founders, the Murphy brothers (1977).

First known as Jelly's Rapids, after pioneer settler Andrew Jelly, the village probably began as a stopping place, a bone-jarring half-day's journey north of Millbridge. Around the site there clustered a school, church, post office, and a few dwellings, and, although unrecorded, probably a mill on the creek, and a hotel. When the post office opened, the new name "Glanmire" replaced the old. But Glanmire's prosperity was short-lived. As the prosperity of the Hastings Road dwindled in the 1860s and '70s, Glanmire faded. A brief flurry of gold-mining activity around the turn of the century failed to revitalize the village.

Today, amid the headstones of a carefully kept graveyard, are the steps to the church; but the church has long disappeared. Where the school once stood on the adjacent lot, only foundations remain. Its new home is now the Millbridge yard of John Norman, grandson of one of the Hastings Road's first settlers, its new function that of storage. These and a few vague cellar holes constitute the only remains of this early village.

MURPHY CORNERS AND THANET

Although separated by two miles of road, these villages performed complementary functions: Murphy Corners, the mill town; Thanet, the stopping place. Murphy Corners, four miles beyond Glanmire, at the intersection of the Hastings Road with a major east-west route, took its name from James and Pat Murphy who settled the southeast corner of the crossroads. By 1860 a school had located there. Until a church was added, 10 years later, worshipping was conducted in the Murphy home. A short distance west hummed the sawmill of A.L. Purdy, which was later operated by the Murphys.

Although no hotel marked Murphy Corners, Thanet, two miles north, became a busy stopping place and boasted no fewer than three hotels. The most notorious was "Thwaites' Place," known throughout central Hastings; J.P. McKillican and S. Menzie offered more sedate accommodation. Like Murphy Corners, Thanet had a school and church and was for a short time a bustling place. But when the depopulation of the Hastings Road brought most activities to a close, the villages fell silent. Little has survived of their palmy days.

At Murphy Corners, the mill, school and church have gone and the Murphy homestead stands vacant. Only one house and a former gas station remain occupied. Of Thanet, only the cemetery has survived.

UMFRAVILLE

Four miles beyond the still active Ormsby, the next centre north of Thanet, lie the few remains of Umfraville. The combination of a crossroads location and a water power site on Egan Creek bestowed on Umfraville growth advantages greater than other villages on the Road. Here, in 1860, William Jorman erected a flour and sawmill, while Benjamin and William Spurr opened a general store. The village soon added a carpenter, shoemaker, church and school. While the Spurrs operated the store until near the end of the century, the other village functions ceased soon after they began.

The rugged old road still twists around the hard granite hills. But, of early Umfraville, only a few abandoned buildings and a stagnant mill pond remain of the short-lived boom days along the Hastings Road.

THE OPEONGO ROAD:

Of Ontario's early colonization roads, the Opeongo has best retained its original pioneer characteristics. Surveyed in 1852 by Robert Bell, by 1865 it was passable from the Ottawa River to Barry's Bay and was considered to be one of the best roads in the Ottawa-Huron Tract.

It was also one of the most thoroughly settled. From Farrels Landing on the Ottawa River, 40 miles west to Dacre, it crosses a level fertile plain, and was settled by Scottish and Irish immigrants. West of Dacre, the road climbs the steep towering wall of Plaunts Mountain, offering spectacular views of lakes and lowlands, and enters the 70-mile chain of hills known as the "Opeongo" or "Black Donald" Mountains. This portion was settled largely by Polish immigrants.

In its early days the road was an important supply route for the lumber men working timber limits in the mountains and a string of villages and stopping places sprang up at frequent intervals. Of these, Renfrew and Barry's Bay grew to be sizeable towns, and Dacre to a small rural village. Most of the others were short-lived hamlets or remained as hotel sites.

Then, in 1893, when J.R. Booth built his railway just a few miles to the north, the timber traffic shifted to the more efficient railway and signalled the end of most of the hotels and of many little hamlets along the road.

The Opeongo avoided the disastrous depopulation which struck other colonization roads and retained many of its early settlers. Indeed, many of its 19th century characteristics—original log barns

Brudenell's old hotel and vacant shop are quiet remainders of busier times on the Opeongo Road (1976).

and homes, lines of snake rail fences and even horses working the fields—survive unchanged. It is a touch of old Ontario that has flourished well into the 20th century.

BRUDENELL

The junction of colonization roads almost invariably spawned strategically placed villages, and the junction of the Opeongo Road with the east-west Peterson Road, 10 miles south of Killaloe Station (at this point called the "Opeongo Junction Road"), was no exception.

By 1871 the Opeongo Road was lined with a string of busy hotels and at this strategic intersection, known first as Brudenell Corners, three hotels were in full operation. Their owners, James Grace, James Whelan and Mme. Desiree Payette, included taverns to quench the thirsts of the boisterous lumbermen. The permanent settlers of the Opeongo Road also required services and the busy intersection soon boasted three general stores, two blacksmiths, shoemakers and carpenters, as well as a church, hall, school and a population approaching 200. Brudenell also enjoyed a daily stage service to Combermere and Rockingham, southwest on the Peterson Road, and to Eganville to the northeast. With the construction of the Booth Line Railway, the railway station at Killaloe became the new stage destination.

In the 1880s the Costello family arrived and soon dominated Brudenell's business community. By 1885, James Costello was operating one of the general stores while Mike Costello opened a blacksmith shop and purchased one of the hotels. Meanwhile Mme.

Payette had purchased John Devine's hotel (originally Whelan's) for a sum of $2,000, while Devine busied himself with the construction of settlement roads.

In 1886 Brudenell was beset by tragedy. One was the death of Thomas Payette, at the age of 33, the other the burning of Mike Costello's hotel. Payette's widow bravely carried on the hotel business for several years; Costello wasted little time in rebuilding that same year.

In 1893, with the extension of Booth's railway, the Opeongo Road villages diminished in importance and Brudenell lost many of its businesses. Only the Costellos remained with the hotel, store and blacksmith shop.

Today the Opeongo Road had been paved between Barry's Bay and Brudenell, and the Peterson Road between Brudenell and Killaloe Station, forming Highway 512. While a few of Brudenell's magnificent buildings, including Costello's old hotel and store, and a fading, frame gingerbread house, still stand at the intersection, none has retained its original function. Most are vacant or used only as residences. With the many empty overgrown lots they testify to the strategic importance of the busy village that once dominated this colonial crossroads.

FERGUSLEA

On a now little-used section of the old Opeongo Road, four miles west of the town of Renfrew, are the remains of Ferguslea. Through the early years of the Road the site was known as "Opeongo," after Thomas Culhane's Opeongo Hotel. Here, the travelling lumbermen could purchase whisky for $2 per gallon, meals at just 25 cents, boots for $1.40, and overalls for $1.00.

When, in the 1880s, the Kingston and Pembroke Railway completed its last leg, Opeongo blossomed into a village. In addition to the hotel, there was a store, sawmill, tannery, school and a string of dwellings along the road. In 1892 the new postmaster, Robert Reid, requested that the village be named "Ferguslie," after the family's sawmill operation on a nearby creek and his father's Scottish home town. For a time Ferguslea thrived, a small but active village.

Just four miles east, at a water power site on the Bonnechere River, lay the growing town of Renfrew. With the increase in concentration of shops and industries in Renfrew, Ferguslea faltered. After several years of stagnation, the village gradually dwindled, and its businesses and residents moved away.

Today, a short distance from the creek, a new lumberyard has replaced Reid's old sawmill. Of Ferguslea's other old buildings, most have fallen silent, several have disappeared and only three remain in use.

THE ROSSEAU AND NIPISSING ROAD:

One of the most completely abandoned of Ontario's colonization roads is the Rosseau-Nipissing Road. So named because it created a 69-mile link between Lake Rosseau (in the Muskoka chain) with Lake Nipissing, its intent was to settle the then virgin territory of central Parry Sound District. Surveyed in 1865, the "Nipissing" Road was completed by 1875. By 1880, many settlers, especially those of German and Swiss

Renfrew County's early logging teams kept the Opeongo Road busy until the opening of the Booth Line Railway in the 1890s provided a more efficient means of shipping lumber.

Weary Nipissing Road travellers, after bouncing their way from the now ghost towns of Rye, Spence or Ashdown, welcomed the rest and repast in the Nipissing Hotel at the Road's northern terminus.

descent, had moved to their free grant lots.

A string of 10 hamlets and villages appeared at millsites and intersections along the road but, of these, only Magnetawan, due to its location on the Magnetawan Canal and to the fertility of surrounding farmlands, reached and sustained a notable size. Two others, Commanda and Nipissing, developed into rural villages, while the others became hamlets.

But the road's heyday was short-lived. The opening of the Toronto to North Bay Railway, in 1886, siphoned most through-traffic, and many farmers, discouraged by the harsh climate and stony soils, fled to Canada's newly-opened West.

The abandonment was almost total. Of the five once-active villages between Lake Rosseau and Magnetawan, none has survived and almost every farm lies abandoned and overgrown. North of Magnetawan, settlement was skimpier, the villages fewer and smaller. Here, too, abandonment was nearly complete; only at the extreme north end near Commada and Nipissing has a viable rural community persisted.

ASHDOWN

The Nipissing Road's most southerly village, Ashdown, developed at the junction of the Parry Sound Colonization Road, a mile west of the village of Rosseau on Lake Rosseau.

Named after pioneer landowners, the village, by 1880, boasted a school, Orange Hall, Methodist Church, a store, and hotel run by the Ashdown family, as well as R.G. Hall's blacksmith shop and A.H. McCann's wagon and carriage factory. A short distance south of the junction, the White Oak Creek provided power for Thomas Scott's planing mill and Cyrus Lawson's sash and door factory. Stages departed daily for Parry Sound to the west for $1.25, and twice weekly along the winding Nipissing Road to Magnetawan for $2, and Nipissing Village for $4.

Ashdown prospered only briefly. The advent of two railways, the Toronto and North Bay line to the east, in 1886, and the Booth Line to the north in 1897, deprived both colonization roads of freight and passenger traffic. With the decline in road use, Ashdown lost its strategic advantage and its businesses moved to the larger village of Rosseau. By 1908 not even the post office remained.

Visible remains of Ashdown are few and scattered; here a log shell, there a frame skeleton, as well as depressions and overgrown yards, indicating old cellar holes and village lots.

NORTH SEGUIN
AND DUFFERIN BRIDGE

As stagecoaches rumbled north from Ashdown, they came first to James Critz's hotel on Ten Mile Lake, then Seguin Falls, a crossroads hamlet at the junction with the Christie Road. (Because Seguin Falls' growth is linked to the building of the Booth Line Railway, its story appears with the saga of the railway later in this chapter). A few miles north of Seguin Falls, the stages came to the villages of Dufferin Bridge, which developed at a millsite, and North Seguin, at a road junction.

Of the former, the *Atlas and Guidebook of Muskoka and Parry Sound* noted in 1879: "The embryo village of Dufferin has a sawmill, store, and hotel." Richard Irwin, G.P. Brooks and Thomas Scott at various times operated the hotel, S. Plumtree, Thomas Vigras and P.J. Vigras the store. Charles Clark was a blacksmith, James Vigras carpenter and Henry Good shoemaker.

North Seguin, just a mile to the north, consisted of little more than a few dwellings and a store and post office run by Art Fry. Half-way

Remains of the Spence Hotel (1976).   **Decaying remains of pioneer homes.**

Much of what was busy Rye now lies in ruins (1976).

between the villages stood an Orange Hall.

As the railways absorbed the former road traffic, and as the population of the Nipissing Road dwindled, these little villages lost their importance and disappeared. Today, other than depressions and overgrown yards, no trace remains. Up and down the road in both directions from the villages, abandoned barns and vacant farm houses tell the sad tale of hardships which drove away many early settlers.

SPENCE

The next stopping place was Spence, at an intersection with the Ryerson settlement road. The junction attracted two stores, a boarding house-hotel, blacksmith shop, two sawmills, a church, a school and several log dwellings.

Most buildings clustered at the northwest and southwest corners, while, dominating the northeast corner, was the two-storey frame hotel, for many years run by Sevitt Simpson.

As the surrounding farm population declined through the early decades of this century, Spence's functions faded. Today the empty old hotel, sagging and weed-infested, continues to dominate the intersection. Vacant buildings, several cellar holes and foundations along the west side of the road testify to the village's former extent.

Just a few miles north, as the road approaches Magnetawan, it suddenly enters a pocket of good farmland. In the heart of Magnetawan village stands a plaque which commemorates the building of the Rosseau-Nipissing Road.

RYE AND MECUNOMA

Although largely abandoned, the Nipissing Road south of Magnetawan is passable year-round; north of that point it becomes little more than a track through the woods.

Near a pocket of farmland, 12 miles north of Magnetawan, the road re-emerges from the forest at the former locations of the stopping places of Rye and Mecunoma. At Mecunoma stood a hotel with the interesting name of "Bummers Roost," which was built in 1882 and burned in 1926. A newer home has since arisen on the old foundations. Two miles north, the village of Rye, named after a town in southeast England, bustled with four hotels, a school and church. Because there were a few farms in the vicinity, Rye likely contained a store and blacksmith shop as well, but no records of these have remained, either on paper or in local recollection.

Today Rye is totally deserted, a victim of the mass flight to the West. The collapsed and decaying hotels and the vacant buildings are curiosities for the children of nearby summer camps. At the time of writing, the attractive white frame church was being dismantled—a disappointing loss of another of pioneer Ontario's vestiges, simple in its beauty, yet once vital to the hardy pioneer community.

North of Rye the Nipissing Road has for several miles been totally reclaimed by the forest.But, close to its terminus near Nipissing, the road, now paved, is well-travelled, the area a prospering rural community.

ADDINGTON ROAD:

Constructed in 1856 by Ebenezer Perry, the Addington Road was to run northward from Anglesea township, in the middle of Lennox and Addington County, to meet the Opeongo Road in Renfrew County. It fell several miles short.

Perry was optimistic as to the future of his road: "The probable future of the settlement? I look forward at no distant day for an industrious, intelligent and rich population—we will have cities where I only anticipated towns, and towns instead of hamlets." Perry's optimism was sadly misplaced. Where the granite and rocks failed to dissuade settlement entirely, it held it to a subsistence level. Even to this day few

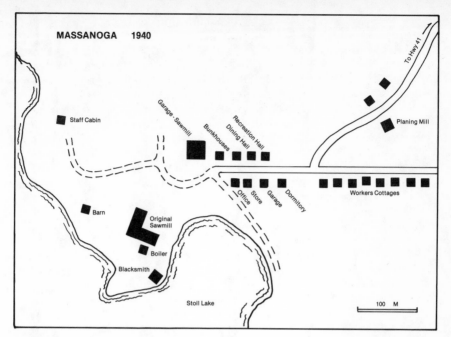

MASSANOGA 1940

Staff Cabin
Garage-Sawmill
Bunkhouses
Recreation Hall
Dining Hall
Planing Mill
To Hwy 41
Barn
Original Sawmill
Boiler
Blacksmith
Office
Store
Garage
Dormitory
Workers Cottages
Stoll Lake
100 M

modern buildings have appeared, save summer cottages where the road skirts the larger lakes.

MASSANOGA

Despite the early rise and decline of settlement along the Addington Road, its only ghost town is of recent vintage. Between 1938 and 1960, on the shores of Stoll Lake, just a mile west of the Addington Road (now Highway 41), stood the prosperous and attractive company mill town of Massanoga.

In 1938, 80 years after the beginning of forest exploitation along the Addington Road, the Michigan firm of Sawyer-Stoll acquired a timber licence for a large portion of Effingham Township. Attempts by the previous owners to ship the lumber westward by rail to Gilmore on to the Central Ontario Railway had bankrupted them. Sawyer-Stoll found trucking the lumber down the Addington Road to Kaladar to be more economical.

On the shores of the lake, the company constructed an extensive mill and village, complete with company office, store, three bunk houses (with the then unique luxury of indoor showers), staff houses and 12 cabins for mill hands and their families. The 200 workers were paid well, the daily wage of $8-10 per day being top pay for the period. They also enjoyed the facilities of a recreation hall which had a pool table, regular movies and dances. In 1942 the company added a school and, for a few years, a post office operated at Massanoga. The milling operations included the sawmill, a boiler room, blacksmith, barns, and a planing mill. In 1945 the planing mill was moved to Kaladar where it could treat lumber arriving by rail from the company's other timber licences in Renfrew county.

After two decades of prosperous operations, bad times struck.

137

A misty morning view of the old Massanoga mill.
The shell of the Massanoga Mill (1975).

Cheaper wood from British Columbia brought a recession to Ontario's lumber industry and in 1962, Sawyer-Stoll reluctantly closed their mill. The workers moved to other villages and Massanoga became a ghost town. A rebound in Ontario's lumber industry briefly revitalized the village until 1974, when a fire devastated the original mill. It was replaced by a portable sawmill but the workers did not return, preferring to commute from their own homes, several miles distant. Then, in 1976, as the portable mill was cutting more timber imported from Renfrew County than local wood, Sawyer-Stoll moved the entire operation to the more productive timber limits near Eganville.

Today Massanoga is but a forlorn relic of its palmier days. Although most of the buildings have been dismantled, several remain; one, the old company office, is now rented to a hunt club. The imposing recreation hall dominated the centre of the one-time village until 1975 when it was dismantled. Now only the shells of the old mill, a few cabins and the one-time store sag sadly in the winds that blow through the forests beside the Addington Road.

Corduroy construction common along many of Ontario's colonization roads was the bane of long-distance travellers used to smoother rides. The burned-over landscape such as this near the Opeongo Colonization Road was a frequent result of the slipshod lumbering practices of the 19th and early 20th centuries.

Construction of J.R. Booth's Railway in the 1890s gave rise to a string of villages, many of which were later abandoned.

J.R. Booth, undisputed lumber king of Ontario in the late 19th and early 20th centuries.

 Chambers' scraper gang busy at work constructing the Booth Line road bed in 1896.

THE BOOTH LINE RAILWAY:

J.R. Booth initiated his ambitious railroad to facilitate the transportation of timber from his vast limits, in the centre of the Ottawa-Huron Tract, to his mills in Ottawa. During the 1890s, the railway was extended to Georgian Bay and eventually carried a greater variety of cargo, including grain, coal and manufactured goods. Booth sold the line in 1905 to the Canada Atlantic Railway Company which, in turn, passed the line on to the Canadian National Railways in the early '20s. Although unrelated to the government colonization road scheme, the Booth Line contained striking parallels. For one thing, its route was almost identical to that originally proposed for the Opeongo Road and, like the colonization roads, the Booth Line gave birth to a string of villages.

Some of these villages depended exclusively upon the railway and collapsed when the railway closed. Others attracted businesses and industries which related to the surrounding population.

In particular, the effects of the postwar recreation boom enabled many villages, especially those in Parry Sound District, to survive the closing of the railway in 1955. Others, in Renfrew County, where the railway still operates, have benefitted from continued prosperity of hinterland activities. Still others, far from the mainstream of recreation, did not fare as well and became the ghost towns of the Booth Line Railway.

MOWAT

On the shores of Canoe Lake, in the popular Algonquin Park, sits a ghost town with its own ghost.

In 1896 the mills and village of Mowat at Canoe Lake were built on the Booth Line Railway as an attempt by the Gilmour Lumber Company to recoup losses incurred through an imaginative but unsuccessful scheme to ship logs from Algonquin Park to mills in Trenton. Their scheme entailed a tedious system of river drives and long portages—a journey of 200 miles, which required 2 full years to complete. By the time the logs reached the mills many had rotted!

The railway location, therefore, had considerably more appeal. By licence, the Gilmour Company was entitled to "326 acres...for a term of 10 years...for the purpose of erecting thereon saw and planing mills together with the necessary buildings and houses to be used in connection therewith ... (They) shall properly survey and lay out in lots and streets on which it is proper to erect workmen's houses... All buildings...shall be of good construction and when made of boards they shall be painted or whitewashed."

The sizeable village included, in addition to the mills, a hospital, school, post office, bunk houses and cottages for the 700 millhands and their families.

The steep, rocky shores of Canoe Lake hindered development of a town plan. Although a few village streets were constructed, most dwellings hugged the western shoreline and that of a small peninsula jutting into the lake between Potter Creek and the portage from Canoe to Joe Lake. Mowat also became an important divisional point on the

Booth's huge mills in Ottawa testify to the extent of this lumber king's timber operations in the Ottawa-Huron Tract.

railway. Beside Potter Creek stood a pump house, water tank and 11 miles of siding. Mrs. Ratan, wife of the railway section boss, spared no effort to keep the nearby station clean. There, for all to see, she hung a sign: "Gentlemen will not, ladies do not, others must not spit on the floor."

Misfortunes continued to plague the Gilmour Company. Barely had the village entered its prime than, in 1898, a slump in the lumber market bankrupted the company. The mills closed and the village was abandoned. In 1905 some buildings were sold for use as private cottages; in 1907 others went to a Kingston salvage firm.

About this time, the reputation of the lakes and climate of the Park were transforming it into a highly desirable recreation area and many lodges appeared. In 1913, on the foundations of the old Gilmour storehouse and boarding house, Shannon and Annie Fraser built the commodious Mowat Lodge. It quickly became a popular resort for city dwellers who, in those days, voyaged to the park by train. Nearby stood the Algonquin Hotel, erected a few years earlier on the eastern limits of the old village, beside the railway station.

Tom Thompson, a famous Canadian painter and one of the "Group of Seven", frequented the Mowat Lodge. From it he ventured in his

143

The village of Mowat, 1928 after construction of the Mowat Lodge.

Mowat's sister lumber milling village, Brulet Lake, survived well past the first war with school, boarding house and several homes only to meet a fiery fate at the hands of the Ontario Government whose peculiar and unfortunate policy it has been to burn down any abandoned historic building on crown land.

favourite grey canoe to paint such memorable masterpieces as "Tea Lake Dam," "Canadian Wild Flowers" and "Moose at Night." On the afternoon of July 8, 1917, Thompson set out to fish. He never returned. Later that afternoon his canoe was found floating in the lake; a week later, his body was recovered. Considerable mystery enshrouded his death and murder was a rumored possibility. In the years that followed, campers have reported a mysterious grey canoe which drifts over Canoe Lake's tranquil, twilight waters, comes to rest on a beach, then disappears, leaving no trace.

144

And so Mowat thrived into the 1920s, not as a mill town but as a resort community. But, in 1930, the second burning of the Mowat Lodge wrote *finis* to Mowat's recreational story. It reverted, in the 1930s, to milling when a steam sawmill operated briefly on the shores of Potter Creek.

Little remains of the old village. The large concrete shell of the more recent mill stands beside Potter Creek, as do a few chimneys and foundations. Irregularities in the ground indicate the location of the old railway siding. Most workers' homes have long vanished, save a couple of the more substantial structures which were originally built for the members of the Gilmour family. A log bridge across Potter Creek, built in 1896 to link the two village portions, now sits, rotting.

The "railway," however, still "transports" lumber. Although the line is closed, the railbed has been graded and gravelled and is now frequently used by noisy, diesel lumber trucks. For, despite the park's designation as a supposed "wilderness" park, lumbering remains a major activity.

In a partial effort to address the wilderness concept, park authorities have decreed Mowat's few remaining Canoe Lake buildings now used as summer cottages be demolished upon the termination of their leases. When that happens the apparition in the grey canoe will be Mowat's only "survivor".

SEGUIN FALLS

Seguin Falls on the Nipissing Road pre-dated Booth's railway by nearly 30 years. In 1873 the village consisted of little more than a hotel, sawmill and post office. Soon the reputation of the hotel spread, causing a contemporary traveller to comment in 1885: "The traveller will find an excellent temperance hotel at Seguin Falls, the proprietor of which, Mr. D.F. Burk, is a most genial and hospitable host, nor should we forget to praise the excellent cuisine of his good lady."

The village also included Adam Fitzer's store and blacksmith shop as well as a church and school, all clustered about the junction of the Nipissing Road with the Christie settlement road.

In 1897 the railway arrived. The older hotel closed and a new hotel, the King George, opened beside the station, about two miles south of the road junction. William Fry, W.S. Morrison and Julius Pearlman all

Seguin Falls' King George Hotel (1964).

opened general stores and a string of dwellings appeared. While the grander homes of the village's wealthier residents nestled amid the shady maples south of the station, north of the station, on a bare rocky ridge, the workers' simple cabins straggled along the road. The village possessed no street pattern, the Nipissing Road being its main and only thoroughfare.

Long after the importance of the Nipissing Colonization Road had declined, Seguin Falls continued to thrive as a major lumber shipping station. In fact, Mrs. Thomas MacKinnon operated the hotel and confectionery well into the 1950s. As the farm population of Montieth township, in which Seguin Falls was located, dwindled from 480 in 1921 to a mere 50 by 1961, Seguin Falls looked more to its railway operation as its sole reason for existence. Then, in 1955, when the rail lifeline closed, the village's residents moved away. By 1960 Seguin Falls' many buildings, save two, stood vacant. The empty church retained its altar cloth and hymnals but heard no more the voices of worship.

Since then, the church, station and several homes have fallen victim to lumber salvors. Yet ample evidence of Seguin Falls remains. Most conspicuous is the handsome two-storey, frame King George Hotel, which is occasionally used by hunters. While the school and a few original homes welcome seasonal occupants, most old buildings bear only silent testimony to Seguin Falls' busy days as a railway town.

SWORDS

Farther west, about half-way between Seguin Falls and Depot Harbour, the railway's terminus on Georgian Bay, there arose another

146

station town. Known first as "Maple Lake Station," the village grew up around a lumber siding built for the Sheppard Lumber Company, a company with extensive timber licences in this part of Parry Sound District. Here the company built a store and several houses, and lured settlers from the shores of nearby Maple Lake.

The influx of tourists coincided with the lumber company's busier days. In 1899 John Sword erected his Maple Lake Hotel, a favourite Canadian "wilderness" destination of American tourists on special trains known as "Buffalo Flyers." Included in their stay was a tour of the Muskoka Lakes, just a few miles to the south. The Buffalo Flyers were discontinued in 1905 when Booth sold his railway to the Canada Atlantic Railway Company.

Through the early decades of this century, the village prospered. A rare pocket of fertile farmland which surrounds Swords retained a sizeable rural population long after the great westward flight at the turn of the century. Thomas Sword operated a general store while P.D. Sword kept the hotel operating and, in addition, acquired part interest in the Ludgate lumbering company. Other stores were run by Mrs. W. Reinner and Rinn and Sanders.

The year 1930 saw official recognition of the Sword family's contribution to the community when the name of the post office was changed to "Swords." When the Swords departed, John Lawson and son assumed management of the general store.

A modern-day ghost town, Swords is almost as well preserved as Seguin Falls. The old weathered store, with house attached, still stands and is partially used as a residence. Beside the store, a string of old company houses peer forlornly from the advancing forests, while, across the road, a new-looking frame house represents the cut-down remnant of John Sword's once busy hotel.

Each summer, Toronto cottagers bring life back to Maple Lake and, during the winters, snowmobiles roar along the former railroad bed, now maintained as a trail by the Ontario government. ●

The former general store at Swords (1975).

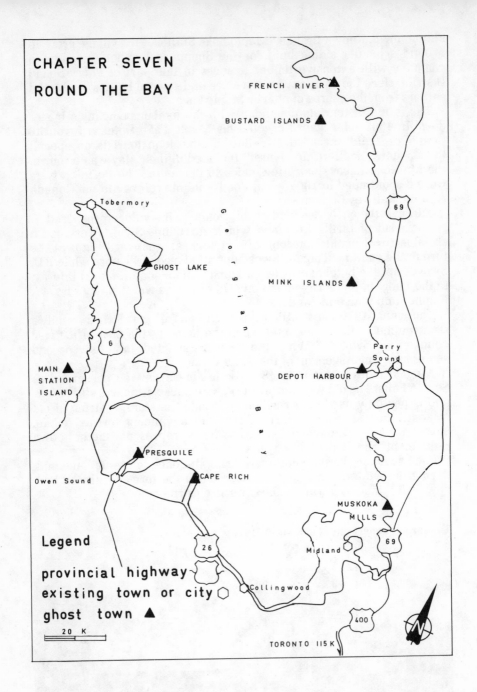

CHAPTER SEVEN
ROUND THE BAY

FRENCH RIVER ▲

BUSTARD ISLANDS ▲

69

Tobermory

Georgian

GHOST LAKE ▲

MINK ISLANDS ▲

6

Parry
Sound

MAIN ▲
STATION
ISLAND

DEPOT HARBOUR ▲

Bay

PRESQUILE ▲

Owen Sound

CAPE RICH ▲

MUSKOKA
MILLS ▲

26

Midland

69

Legend

provincial highway

existing town or city ⬡

ghost town ▲

Collingwood

400

20 K

TORONTO 115 K

N

7

'ROUND THE BAY

Large enough to earn the description as the "Sixth Great Lake," Georgian Bay has a geology as varied as its history. Its most outstanding shoreline is that of the Bruce Peninsula on the west, where the towering limestone cliffs of the Niagara Escarpment peer down upon sweeping capes and tranquil bays. Along the southern shore, long and deep preglacial valleys carved into the Escarpment have created deep protected harbours. The Bay's eastern shore consists of a perilous and confusing maze of an estimated 100,000 islands and shoals, the pink granite of the Canadian Shield contrasting starkly with the clear blue waters. Dominating the northern shore are the dazzling white La Cloche Mountains.

Although the playground of recreational boaters since the 1950s, Georgian Bay, in the 1800s, was all business. From its early role as highway for Indian bands and fur traders, Georgian Bay evolved into a busy scene of fishing, lumbering, and shipping. As a result, many little villages appeared around the Bay, some dependent on lumbering, some on fishing, others on steamships. Those which combined these functions or received the railway, grew beyond single industry villages to become important towns. Those which continued to rely upon just one industry rose and fell with the fortunes of that industry.

149

LUMBERING DAYS:

Although some lumbering occurred on the Bay prior to 1855, it reached boom proportions in the 1880s. By then, the construction demands of the burgeoning American West had drained the timber supplies of Michigan's forests and American eyes turned to the vast, untapped forests of Georgian Bay's hinterland.

The first thrusts of tree-felling failed to produce many milling villages on Georgian Bay's Canadian shores. Logs were bag-boomed and towed, uncut, directly to the Michigan mills. Although a small proportion of timber continued to feed the older mills on the southern shores of Georgian Bay, Canadian residents grew increasingly concerned over the draining of native timber resources to fill American pockets. The Canadian government, fearing American reprisals, refused to impose either tariffs or export taxes. However, in 1897, when the Americans placed a tariff on Canadian sawlogs, but not on uncut logs—a move designed to further speed the American consumption of Canadian forests—the Ontario government was forced into action. In 1899 it passed a regulation requiring that all logs felled in Ontario be sawed in Ontario.

This brought a rush of American mills to Georgian Bay's northern shores and lumbering villages sprang up overnight.

So thorough and so rapid was the devastation of the forests that, by 1905, the lumbering peak had passed and the industry was in decline. By 1940 it was dead.

FRENCH RIVER

A two-mile-wide maze of rocky channels which constitute the mouth of the mighty French River saw the rise of the large, but short-lived, mill town of "French River". Despite terrain that was adverse to construction and situated a great distance from American markets, the site on the main channel of the French River estuary afforded access to a vast treasury of timber.

Prior to 1898 a small summer settlement had existed at the site to boom logs for the American mills. Following the erection of the Ontario Lumber Company mills, in 1898, a thriving town of 250 burst into existence. In addition to the two sawmills, there were the Queens Hotel, two stores operated by S.A. Webb and Company and J.W. Jeffrey respectively, two churches, Presbyterian and Roman Catholic, and S.H. Davis' fishing company. Several crude frame homes lined the short, dirt road which led only a few hundred yards inland from the wharf.

In their heyday the mills presented an awesome spectacle, as J.C. Hamilton discovered on one trip in the 1890s: "Next day we visited French River...a great lumber centre with two mills, immense piles of pine boards and long elevated tramways for the removing and hauling of lumber." So massive were the log booms surrounding the mills that the regular steamers were often prevented from making their scheduled stop.

About this time Georgian Bay was becoming popular as a summer recreation ground. Tourists, lured by the romance and beauty of the Bay's islands and waters, began to frequent lumber company hotels.

The view along French River's main street presented a barren aspect.
French River lumber village as viewed from the steamer dock circa 1900.

An 1892 advertisement in the Parry Sound *Colonial* promotes the "Queens Hotel, French River: Tourists will find this is a first-class house. Good fishing and shooting in close proximity. The wines, liquors and cigars are the best. Billiard Room and Barber shop in connection."

Bare, rocky terrain and isolation prevented any settlement that was unrelated to the milling operation. Thus, a decade or so later, when the mills closed and the millworkers left, the village of French River died.

Due to its isolation the mouth of the French has largely escaped the tourist boom. Aside from a few fishing camps and marinas scattered among the rocky islands, the area has remained relatively unaltered over the decades since the closure of the mills. At the site of the one-time village there remain the sunken boilers of lumber company tugs and a few stone walls and foundations, overgrown by bushes and weeds.

This rare photo of Muskoka Mills testifies to the sizeable nature of this early Georgian Bay operation.

MUSKOKA MILLS

Amid the now popular islands of southeastern Georgian Bay, at the mouth of the Musquosh River, stood the early mill town of Muskoka Mills, one of a concentration of mill towns in that portion of Georgian Bay that prepared wood for the Ontario and Michigan markets.

In the 1850s the Muskoka Milling and Lumber Co. harnessed the waters of the Musquosh River to drive their three sawmills. While most of the dwellings ringed the shores of the little bay where the mills stood, many others were scattered along the coastline towards Franceville, where a hotel stood for a number of years. Normally the mill employed 200 hands but, during peak periods, this doubled to 400. During the 1880s A.H. Campbell was the company president and kept his headquarters several miles to the south, at the inland village of Coldwater.

Stalking the great pines of the Muskoka River watershed, the mill hands cut the timber through the fall season; during the winter they piled the logs on the river ice and waited for the spring break-up and log drive.

These dangerous spring drives created heroes and martyrs. One was Sandy Gray, boss of a Musquosh River driving gang. On a Sunday morning, ignoring the Sabbath, he claimed prophetically: "Boys, we'll break the jam or breakfast in hell." He freed the key log but the jam broke so quickly it carried him to his death over the falls which were subsequently named after him.

Competition with the fishing industry almost cost the company dearly in what must have been one of Ontario's first pollution prosecutions. In November of 1884 the federal government accused the company of allowing excessive sawdust to fall into the fish spawning grounds of the Musquosh River. Mill foreman Truman Aldrich was called before the federal overseer at Victoria Harbour and fined $50. The company, however, appealed the conviction on the grounds that it was impossible for more than small amounts of sawdust to trickle through the floor boards of the mill. Ultimately the appeal was successful and the conviction quashed.

Initially Muskoka Mills could draw from the entire Muskoka River watershed for its timber. That advantage disappeared with the settlement of the interior portions of Muskoka District during the 1860s and 1870s, and in particular with the erection of no fewer than 17 mills near the town of Gravenhurst. Its hinterland and timber supply shrunken, the operations at Muskoka Mills soon dwindled and the century ended with the mills closed.

Around the mouth of Musquosh River a few remnants of Muskoka Mills can still be found. These include the foundations of the mills and a few old company buildings which stood until recent years. Along the shoreline, there remain a few of the old cabins which once housed hardy mill hands and their families. Perhaps the most interesting of all is the crumbling, yet jealously guarded, shell of the old Franceville Hotel, so dilapidated that its days are surely numbered. From the waters by the hotel divers have salvaged the sunken remains of old wooden boats which once chugged between the hotel and the mainland at Honey Harbour.

Today the waters around Honey Harbour abound with speeding motorboats and its islands and shores are congested with summer cottages; while, in a quiet back bay by the mouth of the Muskoka River, nature is slowly reclaiming the one-time mill village of Muskoka Mills, once the hub of activity for the area.

GHOST LAKE MILL

The Bruce Peninsula, largely popular as a recreation area today, depended almost entirely upon lumbering in the 19th century. The forests of this long, narrow limestone projection into Lake Huron's waters, 150 miles northwest of Toronto, were still largely virgin in 1881 when Horace Lymburner and his son Robert landed near Cape Hurd. With an expert eye for lumber, Lymburner immediately recognized a forest which could supply a mill for 25 years and a lake which could supply the water to drive the mill wheels.

Ghost Lake is one of nature's mysteries. Perched on the brink of the 200-foot high Niagara Escarpment overlooking Georgian Bay, the lake was believed by the local Indians to be cursed. But Lymburner was interested neither in natural science nor Indian curses. On a narrow gravel beach beneath the cliff, he set about constructing his mill, a house, and cottages for the mill hands. To direct the lumber down the cliff, he constructed a trench from the lake to the brink, and from there a 55-degree angle flume down the Escarpment's craggy face. To catch the logs as they cascaded over the cliff, he excavated a basin in the beach. On Ghost Lake a small tug drew logs to the flume.

The "curse" of Ghost Lake struck quickly. The *Nellie Sherwood*, the first vessel to carry Lymburner's lumber, set sail from the mill and vanished. Such a fate, however, was not unusual in the tormented waters of the Georgian Bay. Despite this brief setback the mill company grew and thrived and, at its peak, was cutting 12,000 board feet of lumber per day and shipping it to Southern Ontario's urban markets

Great piles of lumber often prevented steamers from making their appointed calls at French River's docks. Sawn timber ready for shipment hides all but the roofs of the village homes.

Crammed into the narrow beach between the foot of the Niagara Escarpment and Georgian Bay's water, Lynburner's Ghost Lake mill busily cut the Bruce Peninsula's timber for 24 years.

via the railways at Owen Sound and Wiarton.

Lymburner's estimate of a 25-year timber supply was just one year off the mark. The mill closed in 1905, 24 years after commencement. By then the Bruce Peninsula had been left a desolate wasteland by the extravagant practices of too many lumber companies.

In 1942 Robert Lymburner revisited his father's old mill: "The mill site is now a forlorn vision of waste—house, cottages and mill all burned. There is no timber of value other than firewood that I know of on the whole peninsula. In the spring of 1920 I spent a month after the snow was gone estimating the assets of the man who bought me out in 1905; I could find only $30,000 worth."

Today some of the regenerating timber shows a more promising future for local lumbering. But at the Ghost Lake Mill, lumbering is history. Only a few pieces of rotting lumber, and the channel cut in the face of the Escarpment mark the site of this formerly bustling mill community.

FISHING DAYS:

Like early lumbering, the pioneer fishing industry on Georgian Bay was both small-scale and local. French Canadian voyageurs who had settled the Penetanguishene area of south Georgian Bay pioneered the industry by catching great quantities of whitefish and trout for local markets. The arrival of the railway at Collingwood in 1855 opened all of southern Ontario to Georgian Bay's fishing industry and ignited a commercial fishing boom.

A new style of fishing vessel invented in 1858 by a Toronto Island boat builder named William Watts, facilitated travel on Georgian Bay's tricky waters. Watts' 20-foot skiff with pointer stern and one or two spritsails was later enlarged in response to increasingly keen competition.

Competition, too, extended the traditional fishing area and brought about the many summer fishing villages or "fishing stations" which came to dot Georgian Bay. Because the major fishing grounds were so far from the fishermen's home bases of Collingwood, Meaford, Cape Rich and Owen Sound, commuting was impossible. They therefore established fishing stations on small, outer islands adjacent to the fishing grounds. Here the fishermen and their families lived from spring breakup until the November 1st closing day. Each station was equipped with warehouses, packing houses and net drying houses. Periodically the 60-foot steam tugs, which also doubled as log-booming tugs, would call at the stations to pick up the crates of fish for delivery to fish buyers. Each crate, stamped with the name of the fisherman, contained 1,200 pounds of fish packed in ice (salt was used at first), trout, whitefish and herring being the most popular species.

These tugs played an increasingly important role in the eventual fate of the fishing stations. Gradually the cabins were enlarged, the decks enclosed, and thus appeared the ancestor of today's "turtle-back" fishing vessels. Permitting longer and more comfortable fishing excursions, the tugs gradually replaced the smaller skiffs and initiated a decline in the use of fishing stations. In the 1950s the proliferation of the lamprey eel in the upper Great Lakes so depleted the stocks that the

These logs are en route down the Musquosh River to the busy Muskoka Mills on Georgian Bay.

A "fort" which wasn't: the remains of the Main Station Island fishing station circa 1905.

rate of fishing which, historically, had been such as to allow fish stocks to regenerate suddenly became "over-fishing." As the prized species disappeared, commercial fishing in the Great Lakes began a long and steady decline.

Today commercial fishing has all but disappeared from Georgian Bay's waters. Gone are most of the fishermen, gone are the mainland fishing centres and gone are the once active summer fishing stations that brought life to Georgian Bay's remote rocky outer islands.

MYSTERY OF MAIN STATION ISLAND

On a small island near the Bruce Peninsula the origins of a mysterious stone building have sparked controversy and spawned legend. Because Baron de Sahontan's map of 1690 showed a military fortification on the island, the legend that the old stone walls were the remains of Sahontan's fort persisted into the 20th century. The truth proved less glamorous for the map showed only a proposed location and the alleged "fort" turned out to be nothing more than a part of Captain Alex MacGregor's old fishing station. After discovering in 1831 that rich fishing grounds surrounded the island, MacGregor established an extensive fishing station and contracted to supply Detroit fish buyers with 3,000 barrels per year of whitefish and herring at $1 per barrel. The island group was called the "Fishing Islands" and MacGregor's headquarters "Main Station Island." So close was the station to the fishing grounds that a lookout in a tree could spot the huge schools of fish and direct the skiffs to them. The huge hauls sometimes took three

157

days to land: "When (they) commenced to feel the pressure of the narrowing of the net the scene was one long to be remembered. There in a small area were entrapped thousands and thousands of fish, sufficient possibly to fill 500 to 1,000 barrels. The water in that circumscribed space seemed to be fairly alive as the fish in their efforts to escape rushed madly about, causing its agitated surface to glitter with their silvery sides."

The fishing community included a huge stone packing house, warehouses and cabins for the fishermen. A harbour on the east side of the island protected their skiffs from Georgian Bay's west-wind furies.

MacGregor was too successful. Three Goderich businessmen, W.S. Gooding, Dr. Wm. "Tiger" Dunlop and Dr. Hamilton, enviously watched his lucrative operation and set out to persuade the government that American interests should not have exclusive rights to a Canadian resource. Their arguments were convincing and the government granted the three exclusive rights to the fishery. Ironically, the new owners still shipped their catch to the Detroit market, but under the flag of their own Niagara Fishing Company.

Whether due to overfishing, or less skill, the Niagara Fishing Company failed and sold out in 1848 to John Spence and William Kennedy of Southampton for a mere 900 pounds. Four years later Kennedy departed for the Arctic. After that the station continued in only intermittent use by fishermen of the Lake Huron ports. It never again operated on the scale that MacGregor had established.

With the drastic decline in fish stocks over the past 30 years, the commercial fishery has departed the Bruce Peninsula. On the once-busy island the walls of the stone "fort" still stand, and of the cabins only a clearing remains on the southeast corner of the island. Rarely do vessels venture into the shoally waters of the Fishing Islands except for recreational fishing or while reliving a portion of Ontario's fishing heritage.

FISHING ISLANDS: THE MINKS

Georgian Bay's 100,000 islands, particularly its outer islands, occur in groups. Here the pink granite knobs of the Canadian Shield approach the surface of the Georgian Bay waters—penetrating it to create island clusters, or hiding dangerously just below it to create the shoally conditions for which these waters are notorious.

About 10 miles west of Parry Sound, the outermost group to pierce the surface, the barren Minks, have barely enough soil to support grass or flowers. On two of the larger islands in this group were large summer fishing stations with ice-houses, net houses, warehouses and about two dozen cabins.

Despite the isolation, or perhaps because of it, life among the community was vibrant. James C. Hamilton commented during his Georgian Bay tour in the 1890s: "We stopped an hour at Kill-bear Point, and after a fine sail, got to the Minks about 9 p.m. The fishermen welcomed us heartily and gave us the use of a shanty, where supper was soon spread. We were invited to the gaieties going on near by, where appeared a house full of a merry party. A visiting fiddler made music, and shoes, not the lightest, beat the floor, not the smoothest, and

Fishing skiffs on Georgian Bay during the 1900s.

happy couples performed as they were called, cotillions, quadrilles and Sir Roger. 'Misery', our amiable musician, brought his guitar, and all went merry as a marriage bell.

" 'Take your places,' 'First couple advance,' 'Promenade all,' were some of the orders of the young fisherman, with broad weather-beaten face, full of enjoyment, who acted as dance master. The guitar's sweet tones aided the fiddler. Little ones dozed in the arms of their smiling mothers, sitting on hard benches, and the rugged features of the men relaxed as they looked on."

Through the early decades of this century, as fishermen turned more and more to the larger tugs, use of the Mink Islands fishing station dwindled. By 1950 only two fishermen remained; soon afterward they too left. Most of the old buildings survived the ravages of wind and weather until 1972 when they were levelled by a particularly vicious windstorm. Today the islands are owned by wealthy cottagers who have converted the net-house into an attractive summer home and have cleaned much of the debris from the wrecked cabins. A couple of sturdy old buildings, the only survivors of fishing station days, still stand on the island's rocky surface while, in the harbour waters, the station's "garbage dump," countless old bottles and other relics await the avid collector.

THE BUSTARDS
Farther north, offshore from the mouth of the French River, sit the flat, treeless Bustard Islands. To most boaters they are but a slim, shimmering line on the distant horizon. But, from 1880 to 1930, the Bustards thrived as one of Georgian Bay's most extensive fishing stations. The ring of islands which formed the cozy harbour contained nearly three

159

An old sketch of the fishing station on the Mink Islands before the turn of the century.

The now silent Bustard Islands on Georgian Bay's northern reaches witnessed the comings and goings of the skiffs and tugs shown here seeking refuge in one of the Bustard's numerous natural harbours.

dozen families and witnessed countless comings and goings of the sturdy skiffs.

For the whitefish, trout and herring, the Buffalo Fish Company, which had an agent stationed in the Bustards, paid $70 per ton. In addition to fish-packing, the Bustard fishermen engaged in oil-making. Boiling down the fish entrails could yield 20-30 barrels of fish oil, valued in Toronto at $10-12 per barrel, per year. James Hamilton witnessed the operation first-hand: "On the Bustards the perfume carried about by an old man from the Lewis Islands proclaimed him master of the vats. He told us in broken English of his cottage, garden and two cows in a pleasant lakeside village, where his good wife had charge in his absence. Nor had he forgotten Stornoway and the herring fishing in his younger days off the Butt of Lewis in his native Hebrides. His calling here had a wonderful interest for the simple-minded old man, and he insisted on our visiting his den. Sitting in an oily scow, he took the oars, and passing out among some islands and into a little bay enclosed with high rocks, we came to a shanty with an iron crane over the doorway, and empty barrels about it. Landing, he ushered us into a crude laboratory. Noisome messes stewed slowly in two iron vats, crude oil rising to the surface. The good man proudly exhibited his apparatus, crane, vats, barrels and stock on hand. He stirred up the simmering rich stuff, in which he seemed as interested and as unconscious of any unpleasantness, as a painter mixing colors on his palette. Alas, our unaccustomed senses could not abide the terrible odors that arose. Waiting till his back was turned, we escaped and were soon breathing purer air on an adjacent mossy rock-top."

The Bustards today are an adventurous destination for the sports fisherman or the history buff. Their distance from shore necessitates cautious navigation and careful reading of Georgian Bay's unpredictable weather. The harbour must be entered directly from the west. Surrounding the interior harbour several vacant cabins, once home to a hardy breed of men, still resist the ravages of wind and weather to remind modern generations of a unique lifestyle long vanished from the Bay.

Smaller fishing stations thrived on dozens of Georgian Bay Islands, Champlain Island just south of the Bustards, and possibly the Snake Islands near Parry Sound as well. The locations of many other one- or two-family stations have been forgotten by the passage of time.

CAPE RICH

Within the boundary of the now abandoned Meaford Tank Range, on a broad, sweeping cape of Georgian Bay's south shore, stood a vital and active 19th century fishing village. From it hardy fishermen ventured in their small "Collingwood skiffs" to fishing banks near and far.

Surveyed into seven blocks by Don McLaren in the 1850s, Cape Rich sprang up on the ground swell of the fishing boom created by new rail links between Georgian Bay and Ontario's urban markets. The McLaren family dominated the village's activities. Don McLaren operated the wharf, storehouse, post office and general store, while Reverend Duncan McLaren offered spiritual guidance.

Fishing was Cape Rich's livelihood. The *Grey County Directory* for

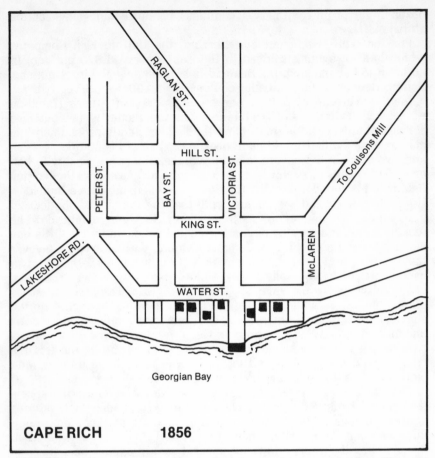

CAPE RICH   **1856**

Map labels: RAGLAN ST., HILL ST., PETER ST., BAY ST., VICTORIA ST., To Coulsons Mill, KING ST., McLAREN, LAKESHORE RD., WATER ST., Georgian Bay

1864 provided this description: "The principal interest in the village is the fisheries. Seven fishing boats are employed, belonging to as many different fishermen, and manned by two and sometimes three hands each. A number of extra hands are employed during the season, who are not considered as residents, and not included in our estimate of the population. As many as 1,200 barrels of fresh fish have been shipped to Collingwood in one season. In 1864, the number reached 800 barrels. Most of these were for the Toronto Market."

Cape Rich played a second role. Settlers moving onto their farm lots surrounding Cape Rich looked to the village for their farming needs. As a result, other businesses located there, including a boot and shoemaker, carpenter, cooper, tailor and a brickmaker who used to advantage the fine local clay soils. Just one mile from the Cape stood Carson's grist and sawmill, built in 1840.

One early family of fishermen were the McInnis', Donald, John and Duncan. Devoted to their trade, they were also the last to maintain the fishing tradition of Cape Rich, as Duncan McInnis continued to ply Georgian Bay's waters almost until the turn of the century.

The fates were unkind to Cape Rich. The larger fishing villages of Owen Sound, Meaford and Collingwood, with their insurmountable advantages of larger warehouses, rail access and fish buyers, made smaller villages like Cape Rich less economical; fishermen abandoned them for the larger centres. Secondly, Cape Rich's agricultural hinterland proved discouraging for the farmers and many vacated shortly after arriving. With no industrial foundation, Cape Rich failed to survive more than a decade into the 20th century.

During the Second World War the Department of National Defence purchased a huge tract of land for a tank range. This tract included the luckless Cape Rich. As a result, the fate which awaited this old fishing village was unique among Ontario's ghost towns. It was the only one to be blown up by our armed forces.

Even today, although the tank range is abandoned, a visit is fraught with danger for, buried under the surface, lie hundreds of unexploded tank shells. This waste of fine recreational land is pitiful.

DAYS OF STEAM:

In 1832 the first steamer to ply Georgian Bay, the *Penetang*, was launched to usher in the steamship age. For several decades steam shipping remained small-scale and local. Then, in 1855, when the Northern Railway opened its Collingwood line, it chartered five sidewheelers to link their terminus with Georgian Bay's small ports.

The opening of farmlands in Manitoba in the 1870s, and in Alberta and Saskatchewan in the 1880s, stimulated steamship activity between Georgian Bay and the Lakehead, while the growth of many lumber and fishing villages around the Bay stimulated local steamer service. Between 1870 and 1900 six major navigation companies came into existence and by 1913 most had merged to form the Canada Steamship Lines. Many Georgian Bay villages grew to depend upon the fortunes of the steamship companies, some as grain handling ports, others as fuel supply ports. Steamers carried passengers, freight and mail and provided many ports with their only link to other parts of the country.

The decline of these ports resulted from a variety of changes which occurred between 1920 and 1960. As the Canada Steamship Lines consolidated its grip on Great Lakes shipping it eliminated duplicate port facilities and introduced larger coal-burning vessels to replace smaller burners. Thus shallower ports and wood-fuel ports were abandoned. As road-building in the 1930s, 40s and 50s brought land access to once isolated ports, steamer service to them gradually ceased, the last being to Killarney in 1962.

Today, while Great Lakes freighters continue to call at Georgian Bay's major ports, carrying grain, oil and iron ore, the only direct descendant of Georgian Bay's steamer service is the car ferry between Tobermory and Manitoulin Island.

PRESQUILE

North of Owen Sound, where the cliffs of the Niagara Escarpment loom over Georgian Bay's waters, a modest gravel spit which juts into the Sound was named "Presqu'ile" or "almost an island." When, in 1873, the increase in steamer activity required more fuel stops, Don Mac-Kenzie saw in Presqu'ile an ideal location for a fuel port. Here, where virgin timber grew close to the water, MacKenzie built a wharf,

The Presqu'ile lighthouse now serves as a camp councillor's quarters (1976).

warehouses and lighthouse and enlisted 75 men and 20 teams of horses to haul cordwood from the forest to the wharf. In 1874 no less than 348 vessels fuelled at Presqu'ile.

Anticipating the growth of a sizeable village, MacKenzie, with the aid of prominent Ontario land surveyor, Charles Rankin, laid out a village plan which, when finished, consisted of four major streets, Wharf, Centre, Main and Water, and extended one-quarter of a mile inland.

Several businesses and homes sprang up in MacKenzie's village. The Gamble brothers opened a general store, William Hays and G.B. Sanders a wagon factory, while Don MacKenzie operated a blacksmith shop. James Sutherland constructed a grain elevator to ship grain produced by nearby farmers. On the south side of the peninsula John MacKenzie erected a sawmill. During the 1880s, Presqu'ile's population peaked at 200 and the village enjoyed both steamer and stage connections.

In 1874 the little port witnessed a gala occasion—the visit of Lord and Lady Dufferin. Although their stop was brief, they were greeted with an elaborate string of colourful lanterns, a huge bonfire, and a gift from MacKenzie of honey produced at local apiaries.

At the turn of the century larger steamers travelled greater distances and coal replaced wood as a fuel for steamers. With this change, Presqu'ile lost its advantage of proximity to fuel. Then the grain elevator burned and was never replaced. By-passed by the steamers, Presq'ile entered a decline from which it never recovered.

The recreation boom which began in the 1920s brought to the shoreline a string of summer cottages. The Presqu'ile site was turned over to a Rotary Club based in nearby Owen Sound and, to this day, offers opportunities for children to enjoy the amenities of outdoor life and local history. Off the northern shore, they can point to the pilings for the wharf. Their camp supervisor now occupies the lighthouse-keeper's old quarters although the light has remained dark for many a decade. The Rotary tuck shop and camp office occupy what was once the old general store. Of MacKenzie's old village streets only a few overgrown paths in the young woods can be traced, while a pair of old village houses still stand—no longer used except by summer visitors.

DEPOT HARBOUR

Depot Harbour, Canada's largest natural freshwater harbour concealed in the maze of Georgian Bay's pink granite islands, did not elude the eye of 19th-century railway builder and lumber baron, J.R. Booth. In 1897 he had brought his Ottawa-Arnprior-Parry Sound Railway to within two miles of Parry Sound village but balked at what he considered were outrageous land prices requested by village land-holders. Undeterred, he decided on a terminus at Depot Harbour on Parry Island, a large Indian reserve separated from the mainland by a narrow channel and only four miles from Parry Sound village.

Realizing the need for on-site facilities, Booth went all-out. He constructed an entire town encompassing a dozen blocks and more than 60 buildings, including homes—both detached and duplex—a school, three churches, a huge boarding house, stores, shops and a 100-room hotel.

Depot Harbour had two functions. As a major railway town it contained a station, water tower, several miles of sidings and a large roundhouse. As a port, it contained a coal dock, warehouses, and a massive grain elevator.

Grand Trunk Railway Engine 2529 at Depot Harbour, 1912.

Part of the thriving port of Depot Harbour, 1925.

The spectacular conflagration of Depot Harbour's elevator in 1945 while it was storing volatile cordite, was one of several blows in the town's demise.

Grain elevators and warehouses at Depot Harbour from the days when it rivalled Ontario's Great Lakes port.

Depot Harbour's large "Island Hotel" circa 1900.

Village homes in Depot Harbour around 1925.

The village lacked little; it enjoyed sidewalks, pumped water, a fire department and a private supply of electricity.

Most villagers were immigrants from no fewer than 11 different European countries and, by 1911, were 650 in number; by the 1920s, an estimated 1,600. Many intermarried with members of the neighbouring Ojibway Indian band and descendants of these unions inhabit the Reserve to this day.

Booth succeeded in his goal of capturing the grain trade. Although he sold the line in 1905 to the Canada-Atlantic railway, grain flowed eastward and manufactured goods flowed westward. Depot Harbour flourished and threatened to outgrow such rivals as Collingwood and Owen Sound.

Then came the devastating 1920s and 30s.

The first blow was the removal of the railway facilities, in 1928, to a new divisional point south of Parry Sound. Depot Harbour lost one of its major reasons for existing as well as many of its residents. Half a decade later, as the dry westerly winds transformed prairie wheat fields into dust bowls, the grain trade dwindled to a trickle and the grain elevator soon fell into disuse. The town faltered and many residents moved away.

A minor revitalization resulted from the construction at Nobel, six miles away, of a large explosives factory to supply the national need in the Second World War, Depot Harbour employees commuting by boat and snowshoe. Cordite for this factory was stored in Depot Harbour's vacant grain elevator and, ironically, wrought the village its final, devastating blow. One night in 1945, fire broke out in the elevator and swept towards the cordite. "The elevator burned like a huge torch," commented a local observer, "and birds of all descriptions flew into the holocaust by the thousands, thinking it was day. The light was so intense that a newspaper could be read at midnight on the streets of Parry Sound four miles away."

After the war most of the remaining residents moved away, leaving behind a dozen streets lined with vacant homes and shops. Although the port continued to ship coal the few workers required commuted by car over the newly-planked railway bridge.

When, during the 1950s, the cottage boom swept Georgian Bay and placed a heavy demand upon local lumber, the CNR sold the buildings—some as cheaply as $25—for cottage construction. Although its buildings have gone, Depot Harbour's relics are perhaps the most extensive of any among Ontario's ghost towns. The railway round-house lurks in the re-advancing forests like a hulking Roman ruin. Concrete sidewalks lie buckled and heaved and, beside them, rusting fire hydrants. Huge maples still line the streets, now shading only rows of foundations, while the winds from Georgian Bay are the only intruders in the once bustling port town. ●

8

THE MINING TOWNS OF EASTERN ONTARIO

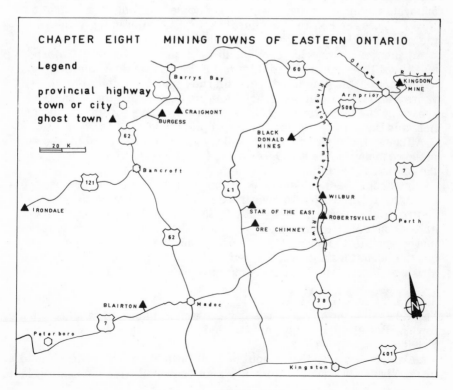

CHAPTER EIGHT   MINING TOWNS OF EASTERN ONTARIO

Legend

provincial highway
town or city ⬡
ghost town ▲

20 K

Barrys Bay

CRAIGMONT
BURGESS

62

Bancroft

121

IRONDALE

62

41

BLACK DONALD MINES

STAR OF THE EAST

ORE CHIMNEY

WILBUR

ROBERTSVILLE

Perth

60

Ottawa River
KINGDON MINE

Arnprior

508

7

38

BLAIRTON

Madoc

7

Peterboro

401

Kingston

In the late 19th and early 20th centuries the rugged hills of Eastern Ontario yielded an amazing variety of minerals. At various times her mines led the country in the production of gold, iron, lead, corundum, graphite and a variety of other minerals. Many deposits, however, were small and easily mined by the pioneer owner who welcomed any supplement to his meagre earnings from wheat and lumber. Occasionally the mineral load was of a sufficient size to entice mining entrepreneurs or mining companies.

Iron was almost as vital as wood for pioneer tools and implements; deposits were eagerly sought and quickly exploited. Ontario's first, albeit short-lived, blast furnace stoked up at Lyndhurst in Eastern Ontario in 1800. Soon many foundries were operating throughout the province. Since most relied on the small ore deposits which occur in peat bogs or "bog ore," their careers were brief and seldom supported a community. In fact, it was the larger rock ore deposits of the Canadian Shield (an old worn-down mountain range covering much of Ontario and Quebec) which gave rise to such iron mining towns as Blairton, Robertsville, Wilbur and Irondale. The major difficulties which faced these operations were transportation (as the hills and swamps defied road transportation, the existence of a railway was a must) and limited size of the ore veins. Rare was the iron mine which lasted longer than a decade.

Ontario's gold rush, although vigorous, gave belated rise to only a scattering of small gold mining camps in Hastings County, north of Belleville. Here, too, small deposits with complicated mixtures of many minerals meant operations were complicated and of short duration. Nevertheless, among the regenerating forests, interesting vestiges of the raucous old camps are yet to be found.

Accidental discoveries brought to light some of Eastern Ontario's most lucrative deposits. Graphite in the Black Donald Mountains and corundum on Mt. Robillard were literally stumbled upon only a few years—and a few miles—apart. Both deposits were large and rich, spawning the boom towns of Burgess and Craigmont in the corundum field and Black Donald Mines in the graphite field.

Although lacking in glamour, lead was once an important ingredient in the economy of Eastern Ontario and for a time the Kingdon Mine was the sole supplier of this nation's lead.

Why should such mineral wealth be peculiar to the eastern portion of southern Ontario? Although the Canadian Shield underlies most of central and eastern Ontario, only in the east did the mixing of rocks and chemicals, aeons ago, produce the vital combinations of ingredients for the formations of various minerals. As the deposits ran out the boom towns generally died and thus Eastern Ontario offers a striking concentration of ghostly mining towns.

GOLD RUSH:

"Gold rush!" These two words conjure up the names of famous boom towns—Barkerville, Dawson City and even El Dorado, Sir Walter Raleigh's lost city of gold.

Unknown to many today, southern Ontario once fell victim to gold fever. Visions of golden grandeur which beckoned from the California

Busy miners in the Ore Chimney Gold mine.

gold fields just two decades earlier also cast their spell from the rugged, rocky hills of central Hastings County, an area north of Belleville.

The Star of the East and Ore Chimney gold mining camps are among the few that have survived since eastern Ontario's golden heyday; to this day they echo to the ring of the gold-seeker's hammer.

It all began on the farm of John Richardson near Madoc: "On 18th August, 1866 I discovered gold on the John Richardson lot..." wrote Marcus Herbert Powell, clerk of the local division court. "I was following a seam of copper...when it suddenly opened out into a cave 12 feet long, 6 feet wide and 6 feet high so that I could stand upright in it. The gold was...in the form of leaves and nuggets and in the roof it ran through a foot thickness like knife-blades. The largest nugget was about the size of a butternut."[1]

By fortunate coincidence an Officer of the Geological Survey of Canada, one A.G. Vennor, was in the area at the time. He studied Powell's samples and proclaimed them to be of "unusual richness."

Scarcely had that winter's snow melted than southern Hastings County began to resemble the frantic gold fields of the West. As frequently as four times a day, stages carrying prospectors, miners,

"Cariboo" Cameron (standing at left) was one of the principal characters in the disappointing Hastings County gold rush.

speculators and swindlers rattled northward from Belleville and Trenton, and a single log shanty exploded into a village of 80 buildings. The village acquired the name Eldorado, after Raleigh's elusive city of gold. The irony was unintentional for the Hastings gold was to remain elusive for a number of years.

Mindful of the lawlessness of western gold towns, the government dispatched a squad of 25 mounted policemen. Immediately upon their arrival, they found their hands full, for the notorious "Cariboo" Cameron had arrived from the West with a number of his gang, marched to the Richardson Mine, and had demanded to see the glittering discovery. Refused entry, they began to tear down the frame building protecting the mine entrance. The horsemen arrived in time to prevent violence by persuading the mine manager to grant Cameron his wish. He was not disappointed.

Lawlessness, unfortunately, did take hold—not in the form of Wild West shootouts, but in salting of claims and dishonest assays. Speculators and prospectors, deluded by fake gold discoveries, lost millions of dollars in worthless investments. Even the experienced "Cariboo" Cameron lost his fortune and returned to the Cariboo, to die a poor man. When the scale of the hoax became known, the bubble collapsed. Even the few genuine claims closed down, defeated by a form of refractory gold ore which could not be separated by contemporary crushing processes.

Not until the end of the century did the invention of cyanide separating permit the milling of the tricky Hastings gold; even then most operations were small-scale. Camps rather than towns developed at the mine heads and, although small, provided dances, motion pictures and other entertainment for the local communities. However, ore bodies were meagre and, one by one, the gold mines closed. Ghost camps which literally dotted the rugged landscape of central Hastings and the neighbouring counties of Lennox and Addington now lie overgrown and forgotten; the tote roads have been reclaimed by the forest.

Rare indeed is the ghost camp that the "explorer" can even reach much less explore. Therein lies the appeal of two accessible and well preserved ghost camps, the Star of the East gold mine and the Ore Chimney gold mine.

Following the perfection of cyanide separating, the Ore Chimney Mining Company sank their first shaft in 1909, discovering and mining veins at seven different levels and eventually descending 400 feet below the surface. A 20-stamp mill put into operation in 1915 was enlarged in 1922, and the nearby Skootamatta River was dammed to provide electrical power. Despite the investment, shareholders became skeptical. One declared the name "Chimney" to be appropriate, for he thought of it as a mine where the "gold goes up in smoke." Another moaned, "I am glad I saw the mine. It has added something to my knowledge. I have seen lead dollars and wooden nut-megs. I have even read the 'Headless Horseman', and now I have seen an oreless mine."

Nevertheless, the camp grew to be one of the largest. Before it was abandoned it contained two bunkhouses, a cookery, three private residences, mine office, assay office, blacksmith shop, power house, boiler house and huge gravity mill. Much of the site has remained untouched. The large wooden headframe still rises above the brush and around the pit are the shell of the power house, the remains of the ore shack and bunk house, and the foundations of the large mill.

Only 10 miles away sleeps the second of the golden ghost camps. Although the Star of the East gold mine operated for a mere four years, 1903 to 1907, two shafts provided a 10-stamp mill with enough material to produce more than 1,000 tons of crushed ore. The site, deep in the bush, still contains, of all things, an old safe firmly embedded in the foundations of the company's office. Nearby lie the bunkhouse foundation and the gravity mill, still with its old wooden flywheel. But the private residences, the stores, barn, icehouse, powder house and blacksmith shop disappeared long ago.

Dreams of gold which inspired the early prospectors may yet persist for the oldtimers say that, amid the tailings or among the rocks, some of the elusive Hastings gold can still be found.

WHEN IRON WAS KING: BLAIRTON

Iron was one of Ontario's earliest mineral products and Blairton was her earliest iron capital.

After construction of the first iron ore blast furnace at Lyndhurst in Eastern Ontario in 1800, others appeared at Normandale, Olynda and other small communities. For a time the ore supply came from peat bogs and was known as "bog ore." Then, on the shores of a remote lake in eastern Peterborough County, the "big ore bed" was discovered. Great chunks of ore blasted from the limestone were carried by scows to blast furnaces, located a few miles east in the village of Marmora. The success of the mine was contingent upon the success of these blast furnaces.

Charles Hayes, an optimistic Irishman, was among the first to undertake the mining and smelting operations. However, the difficulties in transporting the bulky ore over the rugged rocks and through the many swamps to the markets on Lake Ontario drove Hayes'

The Great Hastings Gold Rush, while a fizzle, did produce small amounts of gold. The scene here may well have resembled that in the Ore Chimney or Star of the East gold mining operations.

costs beyond his profits. The property changed hands several times but the transportation obstacles defeated every effort. Even Ontario's "Iron King," Joseph Van Norman, founder of iron furnaces at Normandale, Hemlock and Olynda in southwestern Ontario, found the area's rugged features too strong a foe and gave up after a few expensive years of operation.

Ultimately the railroad saved the day for it provided a much cheaper means of moving the ore. In 1866 the newly formed Cobourg, Peterborough and Marmora Railway and Mining Company built a spur line to the iron deposit and, a year later, the mine finally began to operate at a profit. A contemporary writer observed: "The mine reopened in 1867 employing 300 miners, and the quiet little village of Blairton named for a Scottish settler has become a bustling community. Forty cottages were built by the company to house the influx of employees, and the settlement now has not only a post office, school, Wesleyan Methodist Church, Orange Hall and railway station, but also a telegraph office, three general stores, two bake shops, three hotels—including the well known Purdy House—two boarding houses and numerous liveries and blacksmith shops." Other hotels were operated by Gilbert Weller and Emman Vaughan. Stephen Goodall supervised the mining operations, James Barber the railway.

The company prepared for a surge of miners by surveying a town with 11 streets and 220 lots. Most were purchased quickly. The busy corner of King and Queen Streets witnessed constant coming and going of shoppers and hotel patrons while, some distance away, past the boarding houses on John Street, came the din and the dust of the ironworks. But even more miners were needed, the Ontario *Gazeteer* for 1869 exclaiming, "even though the land is almost all taken up miners and labourers are in great demand." Soon the population exceeded 500 and Blairton's fame grew world-wide, for this boisterous and dusty mining town deep in Ontario's remote rocklands had become the largest iron producer in the country.

But transportation continued to be an expensive burden and when water unexpectedly began seeping into the pits, the cost of operation became prohibitive. In 1875 the mine closed. Within 9 years the town's population had dropped from 500 to 100 and only two hotels, two stores, the school and the church survived the closure.

Expectations lingered nevertheless. In 1884, C. Blackett Robinson wrote: "Blairton is not nearly as prosperous as it was when the iron mine was being worked but the opening of the Ontario and Quebec Railway will, it is hoped, restore things to their former state."

Sadly the new railway did not revive the mine. By 1906 Blairton's population had dwindled to a mere 25 and, of all the commercial activity of the 1860s and '70s, only Tom Caskey's general store survived.

Few of the original houses have weathered the years. Now, at the over-grown corner of what were King and Queen Streets, the foundations of Caskey's old store appear above the weeds. The railway bed is still traceable but only just; John and George Streets are long over-grown, shrubby fields hiding the foundations and lot lines. Canada's one-time "iron capital" gains new life each summer when cottagers and tenters flock to the shores of nearby Crowe Lake.

One of Blairton's few original mining structures to survive the turn of the century.

Sketch of the mine and tramway at Blairton during its operating years (from: ILLUSTRATED HISTORICAL ATLAS OF THE COUNTY OF PETERBOROUGH).

Blairton was, at its peak, Canada's largest iron mine and required such equipment as the "Big Derrick" shown here under assembly in 1872.

IRONDALE

In a remote and rugged part of Haliburton County, the iron mining town of Irondale sputtered into existence amid a muddle of frustrating and futile iron mining ventures.

The first settlers to the area had been forced to pick their way along the new Monck "Road" which, badly misnamed, was little better than a vague trail through the bush. Some of the pioneers halted on the sandy banks of Devil's Creek and the Irondale River to hack their homesteads out of the primeval forest.

One pioneer, W. Robinson, struck iron while clearing his lot; shortly afterward, J. Campbell encountered a like deposit.

Within a few short years a series of rag-tag mining ventures swung into action; the first iron deposits were quarried and hauled by wagon along the rugged Monck Road to the railway at nearby Kinmount. In 1881 an adventurous Irishman named Miles built a branch line from the railway north of Kinmount, seven miles to the iron deposits, but, after shipping a few carloads of ore, found himself bankrupt. Then two Americans, Parry and Mills spent over $200,000 on a smelting furnace and equipment, only to lose everything by fire.

Still they came. In 1881 Charles Pusey and L.B. Howland formed the Toronto Iron Company and discovered further iron deposits. Their plans, the most ambitious to that date, entailed a labour force of 500 men and two blast furnaces which would turn out 22,000 tons of pig iron per year. Their scheme was partially realized.

Because local farmers were so busy cutting cordwood for the furnaces and tending to their farms, Pusey and Howland were forced to import 300 Italian workers to quarry the ore and operate the smelter.

Long-time residents treated the mining prospects with some skepticism, as the Minden *Echo* of March 12, 1885, reveals: "The iron business is moving very slowly. As the 'inquisitive boy' would say, what

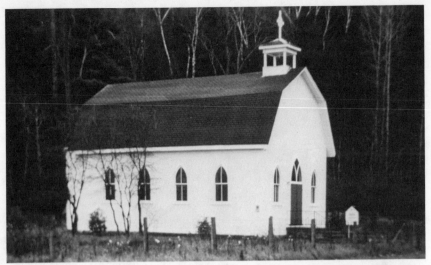

Charles Pusey's handsome church stands in Irondale to this day (1975).

is the reason? Because the men think they are working for a dead horse. What makes them think so? Because they have worked for the same before. A former correspondence in the *Echo* says the miners were going to work with the company's old broken down engine; but unfortunately (or fortunately) they had to throw it out because it refused to do its work.''

On the sandy banks of the river, the town of Irondale was surveyed and a brief boom followed. Miles' railway was extended through the area to Bancroft and renamed the Irondale and Bancroft Railway. In addition to the company offices, boarding houses and miners' cottages, Irondale gained two general stores which were operated by Charles J. Pusey and Peter Barr, an earlier settler. S.E. Hancock was the village smithy for many years and W. Checkley, the shoemaker. In 1889 Pusey built the beautiful white frame St. John the Baptist Church which stands to this day. The Iron company operated until 1900 when the deposits finally ran out. As the mine closed and the workers migrated to greener pastures, the village's population slipped to fewer than 50. Many farmers too were forced to leave for the miners had been the major market for their produce. Nonetheless a small farm populatioin lingered, surviving by shipping lumber on the new railway to mills at Kinmount and Gooderham, or outside the area, and allowing Barr's store and Hancock's smithy shop to operate for several years after the mine's demise.

In 1951 James Howland placed, in the pretty church which Pusey had built, a tablet cast of iron from the old mine and dedicated to his grandfather, C.J. Pusey.

The photogenic little church stands in stark contrast to the vacant houses and weedy foundations that once were Irondale; the iron pit, on a rugged ridge overlooking the site, is filled with water. In 1960 the railway closed and the tracks were lifted (to be made into razor blades). The station master's house, however, remains occupied.

The scenic landscape and the waters of nearby Salerno Lake have attracted cottagers and, although the halcyon days of the iron mining will never be repeated, each summer does bring a significant, if temporary, burgeoning of Irondale's population.

ON THE OLD "KICK AND PUSH": ROBERTSVILLE

From the rugged, inaccessible hills of northern Frontenac County, valuable iron deposits taunted mining companies for years. It was not until the 1880s, when the Kingston and Pembroke Railway Company pushed their rails across the swamps and into these rugged hills, that these deposits became economical.

The beginning of Robertsville is shrouded in mystery for no record of its beginning has survived, although exploration and quarrying must have begun sometime after construction of the KPR in 1880-1. Early efforts were only moderately successful for, as the Renfrew *Mercury* of 1884 reported, the first Robertsville mine, known as the Lizzie, had shut down by 1883. Then, following the discovery of larger and more valuable ore veins in 1884, Robertsville developed into a sizeable mining community. In 1888 the Ontario *Gazeteer* recorded no fewer than 200 persons living at Robertsville. In addition to the miners, there were a number of carpenters, blacksmiths, shoe-makers and a general store operated by J.W. Douglas. The company also operated a store and office.

Robertsville's only remaining resident, Alex White, recalls the appearance of the town when 28 "duplex" houses lined both sides of a road in what is now a field, while the company store, office, and boarding houses lay beside the railway spur at the end of this road. And from the little range of hills just beyond, rose the clatter of the quarry and the head frame of the shafts.

Because mining techniques were crude, the Robertsville Iron Mining Company shipped only 7,000 tons between 1887 and 1895. In 1901, its last year, the mine shipped 6,000 tons via Kingston to the mills at Sault Ste. Marie and then fell silent, the iron depleted. Flurries of exploration in later years revealed little and Robertsville quickly faded from the maps.

Although trains continued to chug past Robertsville, the town was a ruin. Shortly after the mine closed, the houses were dismantled and the wood used elsewhere, leaving, as evidence, only vague mounds in a field. The company store, office and boarding house stood for several years; the foundations are still quite fresh. Evident too are the KPR spur lines and the minesite. The only true survivor is, ironically, a neat little pioneer and miners' cemetery which seems strangely out of place amid the blowing grasses of a nearby pasture.

The pastoral little valley which greets the eye today is surely a contrast to the noise and bustle which emanated from its confines 80 years ago.

WILBUR

Because the track of the Kingston and Pembroke Railway line twisted

The mining operation at Wilbur.

Wilbur, the minehead and talus heap around 1900.

so sharply through north Frontenac's rugged hills, the old steam engines had little chance to display their full power. Railway riders using the line's initials, K & P, nicknamed the line the old "Kick and Push." Puffing northward from Robertsville, the KPR engines would stop at the attractive valley villages of Mississippi, Clarendon, Snow Road, and then Wilbur.

Wilbur, like Robertsville, sprang up when the railway gave access to a substantial iron deposit. With its large reserve of ore, it became the leading iron producer on the KPR. By 1888 it had some 250 residents, most of them miners toiling for the Kingston and Pembroke Iron Mining Company. More than just a company town, Wilbur included Dave Tait's blacksmith shop and William Caldwell's general store, as well as a shingle mill, carpentry shop, and shoe emporium.

A Renfrew Mercury, dated May 5, 1887, reported: "The chief pit at the mine of Wilbur is 220' deep. The daily output of ore was about 100 tons per day. The capacity will be increased to 250 tons by improvements to machinery." The report added that the American syndicate which owned the iron deposits along the KPR boasted land holdings in excess of 15,000 acres. The Wilbur mine was their most productive, shipping an estimated 125,000 tons of ore between 1886 and 1900.

The hilly terrain forbade a neatly designed town. Instead the houses and shops lined two sides of a road which twisted across the tracks and on to the mine, a quarter of a mile away. A few buildings lay alongside the track itself. By the lake near the mine stood two bunkhouses.

One winter night in 1887 the mine experienced tragedy, the Renfrew Mercury of February 25 reporting: "Terrible Mining Accident. Five men crushed to death in Wilbur mine on KPR. The following is the latest account of the Wilbur mine accident. At 1:30 a.m. a huge slide of earth weighing many tons was without an instant warning precipitated from the roof upon a number of miners who were working around the skip car. Those who escaped death sounded the alarm which was quickly responded to and the work of rescuing those alive and recovering the bodies of those killed began. Five men were directly under the centre of the mass where it fell and all were taken out dead. Long before the bodies were recovered the wives, children and other relatives of the unfortunate dead had assembled at the mine and many heartrending scenes occurred."

In 1900 William Caldwell, the storekeeper, acquired the mine and operated it for seven years before selling to the Wilbur Iron Ore Company. Under the presidency of one Dunbar, this venture lasted only four years. The deposit was dwindling and, in 1911, the mine closed.

As the miners and businessmen moved away Wilbur became a ghost town. Bereft of a market for their produce, local farmers also moved out and the roads to the old village fell into disuse. It was not until recent years, when recreation authorities gravelled the abandoned KPR railbed, that easy access to Wilbur was restored.

The scene today is cluttered. While a few old houses and other abandoned buildings still stand, most of the houses and places of business have degenerated into foundations, cellar holes and scattered lumber hidden by advancing underbrush. Rustling hulks of old cars

The mine buildings at Craigmont during its years of operation.

peer above the tall grass, marking an automobile graveyard. When the railway tore down the station, one resident moved the station name-board to his own home so that today, as in the past, there is a sign of welcome to the village. But, alas, it is a village without people.

THE CORUNDUM BOOM:
CRAIGMONT

Once the world's largest producer of corundum, the ghost town of Craigmont now sleeps quietly in the shadow of Mt. Robillard.

Before the opening of the mine, the stillness of the mountain was broken only by the early pioneers. Because the nearby York River marshes contained large quantities of cranberries, many settlers visited the mountain to pick the berries. It was after one such expedition, in 1876, that Henry Robillard and his daughter noticed rocks resembling, the girl thought, cruet stoppers. Local "experts" initially proclaimed them to be phosphate and it was not until 1896 that W.T. Terrier of the Canadian Geological Survey identified a huge deposit as being that of the hardest materials known to man—corundum. Since only diamonds are harder, corundum was in great demand as an industrial abrasive. Excited by the discovery, mining magnates formed The Canadian Corundum Company and lost little time in leasing 1,400 acres on Mt. Robillard. Not waiting to erect new buildings, they refitted an old water powered sawmill with crushing machinery and constructed a town to house miners and managers, naming it after B.A. Craig, the company's first vice president. Thus, in 1900, Craigmont was born.

The new community acquired amenities similar to those of older towns. A community hall, complete with stage, witnessed dramas and fashion exhibitions from far and wide. The children had the benefit of a school and the wives the benefit of what was at that time a luxury, the telephone. There were, in addition to the company store, several private enterprises, including stores, two tailors, a barber, a photographer, and, for a time, the services of Dr. J.L. Poirier, a surgeon from St. Michael's Hospital in Toronto.

The town developed in two sections. The eastern section included the company's stores, offices and boarding houses, and lay under the shadow of the dusty mill and the noisy quarries. The western section, containing the school, church, private businesses and homes, enjoyed a quieter atmosphere a quarter of a mile away from the mining and milling operations. Here, boardwalks protected skirts and trousers from the muddy perils that the dirt roads presented each spring.

But, to the chagrin of the hard-working miners, the town lacked what was, to them, one of life's requirements—a tavern. Since the company had decreed that Craigmont would be dry, the thirsty miners had to trudge five miles along the "high road" to Combermere, a nearby lumber town, on Sundays, their only day off, to satisfy the thirst brought on by frequent 12-hour shifts. For non-walkers, a thrice-weekly stage linked the two communities.

By 1904, 200 miners were at work in the mines and the mill; two years later this doubled to 400. Because most of the local populace could at best supply only seasonal labour, the company was forced to rely on labourers imported from Europe. The mine's manager, H.E. Haultein, reported: "The local labour supply is small and very irregular, depending upon the season and the harvest, and the supply is kept up by importation, not quite so systematic or so coercive as the Transvaal but still containing all the unsatisfactory elements of labour importation." He reported that, of the 260 employees at the mill, only 2 had prior knowledge of concentrators.

The Craigmont mill had the largest ore crusher in Canada and, single-handedly, accounted for 80 per cent of this nation's corundum production. From high on Mt. Robillard the regular echo of explosions signalled the start of the crushing and milling process. Each blast would liberate 3,000-4,000 tons of ore. Stoneboats dragged the crushed rock to a tramway which in turn carried the ore into the upper portion of the mill. A "wet process" of separation forced the heavier corundum to separate itself from the lighter associated rock. The corundum then travelled over rollers to the drying room where mill workers waited to hand-separate it into 18 different sizes and pack it into "100-pound" bags. Following this operation a tramway transported the bags to barges waiting at a landing on the York River. The next stop was the railway at Barrys Bay, on the north end of Kamaniskeg Lake, whence the corundum made its way to a variety of foreign destinations. The year 1906 saw 2,914 tons of finished grain corundum thus leave the Craigmont mill.

The town grew, prospered, and was clearly a community full of vitality and optimism. Then, on a cold February night in 1913—disaster. The mill was ablaze.

Despite fast work by the miners, the flames quickly spread and destroyed the entire mill. Within hours, 150 mill workers had lost their jobs. Although milling operations shifted to the neighbouring town of Burgess, a sister corundum mining town, the workers began to drift

Panorama of the town of Craigmont when corundum was king.

away, some moving to Canada's burgeoning west, others to the new mines of Northern Ontario. Despite intermittent activity until 1921, Craigmont became a ghost town.

Although the old "high road" from Cobermere to Craigmont is now impassible, visitors reach Craigmont via a newer paved road on its western limits—and indeed many come.

Each summer rockhounds converge from across the continent to scour the rocky face of Mt. Robillard or pick through the tailings below in search of prized corundum crystals.

Although the boardwalks and most buildings have long vanished, vestiges of the old town still reward a search through the fields and young bush. Evidence of the huge extent of the boiler room, concentrator and grader are found in the cement foundations, pillars and walls on the lower slopes of the mountain. Two old houses remain; one used in the fall by a hunt club, the other, a quaint and attractive log house, occupied by—so the locals say—a self-styled monk. Several foundations, some fresh, some mere grassy mounds, dot the old road sides. At the town's western extremity the school gate swings in the breeze while weeds grow up amid the old foundations.

Quiet has returned to Mt. Robillard, a contrast to the days when corundum was king.

BURGESS

Although overshadowed by her more famous sister-town of Craigmont, Burgess Mines also reached considerable proportions during Canada's corundum boom and, despite smaller deposits, operations at Burgess Mines actually outlasted those at Craigmont by four years.

Mining activity commenced in 1902 when the Ontario Corundum

184

One of the mine buildings at Burgess Mines.

Little of Burgess Mines has survived the ravages of time (1975).

Company began quarrying from a steep cliff face and shipping hand-picked ore to the United States for further concentration. Only after the company erected a mill could concentration occur at the mine site. A modern mill, it contained five Blake crushers, two impact crushers, a magnetic separator and several pneumatic jigs. By 1907 miners were busily quarrying six cuts in the mountainside.

By then the town had become a thriving community—smaller than Craigmont, but no less active. The *Ontario Directory* for 1908 quotes Burgess Mines' population as being 200. When fire closed the mills at Craigmont in 1913 Burgess received an influx of miners from that dying village and the population surged to 300. While many lived in the boarding houses or the hotel, miners with families were provided with

Amusement Hall, Black Diamond Mine, provided miners with a welcome change of pace from the mine and mill.

small cottages. Choice of worship was limited, for the town had only a Methodist church, while a post office and telegraph office provided links with the outside world. Like Craigmont, Burgess Mines was a dry town and to quench their thirsts miners travelled the several miles to Combermere or Maynooth.

The first automobile in Burgess Mines caused a considerable stir: "When Robert Stringer, a store owner and blacksmith near Stringer Lake drove the first car in the district in 1913, some of the more daring miners at Burgess Mines offered him a dollar to take them on a tour of the community. Stringer agreed, and the group had a ride, although some of the more timid miners backed away, fearing that the vehicle might blow up."

In the end, technology doomed Burgess Mines. While the Burgess Mills continued to crush Craigmont's ore until 1917, a cheaper synthetic substitute named "carborundum" had been placed on the market. Unable to compete with the cheaper synthetic, the company closed its mill.

Faced with little in the way of alternative employment locally, the miners and their families drifted away, leaving in their wake yet another ghost town to wither in Ontario's once-famous corundum fields.

 The shafts where these sweating workers posed were subject to several floods from the waters of Whitefish Lake just over their heads.

One of the many disasters to beset the Black Donald Mines, a fire in 1912.

Access to the site today is via the New Carlow road, south of Highway 62, a few miles east of Maynooth. There the visitor will find ample evidence of the former mining and milling activities. The walls of the crusher peer through a forest of young birch trees while, across the rutted road, stand the log remains of a storage building. A quarter of a mile away, beyond the talus heap, lies the quiet meadow where grassy mounds tell of miners' homes and a once bustling community. On the rocky hill above are the scars of the six quarries which fed the mills.

Perhaps in the Maynooth pub, still the only drinking establishment for many miles around, the visitor may find older residents who can remember when thirsty miners from the Burgess Mines would walk those seven miles for their liquid refreshment.

ACCIDENT ON WHITEFISH LAKE: BLACK DONALD MINES

In 1889, when John Moore slipped on a mossy rock beside Whitefish Lake, little did he realize that he had uncovered Ontario's richest graphite deposit—one which would produce continuously until 1938, and intermittently until 1954. In 1890 the Ontario Graphite Company acquired the site and, in 1896, began extracting and milling.

After just five years of operation the waters of Whitefish Lake burst through the roof of the shaft—the first of several such incursions. Following the vein under the lake the drillers had excavated the shaft so close to the bottom of the lake that the weight of the water collapsed the thin rock roof. The shaft flooded and the mine closed.

This tempting deposit would not long lie idle. In 1904 Rinaldo

McConnel, owner of a graphite operation at nearby Olivers Ferry, on Big Rideau Lake, attempted to pump the flooded shaft but failed. Then a new firm, the Black Donald Graphite Company successfully resurrected the operation and led the mine to its most successful period. With the First World War came demands that entailed more elaborate machinery. Soon a 30- and a 75-horsepower engine went into operation at the refinery, powered by a 400-horsepower generating plant on the rapids of the nearby Madawaska River.

Taking advantage of a spectacular view of Whitefish Lake, its sparkling waters dotted with islands and the Black Donald Mountains looming in the background, the company constructed a comfortable town. To provide the best living conditions the company offered the 105 workers and their families rent-free homes, complete with gardens; to offset the hardships of isolation and double shifts brought on by war demands, they added a community hall with stage and screen; and to complete the gamut of village amenities included a church and school. At its peak, during and after the First World War, the village boomed to 77 buildings and more than 200 residents.

In those days the Black Donald product was well-known. A common sight was a yellow tin of "No. 2 Fine Flake" with a kilted Highland piper on one side and, on the other, these instructions: "Add five to ten per-cent to greases, one to five percent of oils, or one teaspoonful per pint of oil. The special function of graphite is to even up the minute irregularities found in all bearing surfaces. Black Donald Flake Graphite is the purest, toughest graphite on the Canadian market and is specially fitted by nature for this particular purpose."

Then Black Donald Mines began a slow decline. Following the war, demand for graphite slumped and the work force shrank to 70. Nevertheless, the townspeople maintained their spirit. Operations continued but, in 1938, the ore supply finally ran out, the mine closed and workers moved away. When another world war renewed the demand for graphite the Frobisher Exploration Company moved in and built a new mill to work the tailings. Then, in 1950, the waters of Whitefish Lake invaded again. The lake burst into the workings "...just like Niagara Falls. The tremendous air pressure blew huge lumps of concrete out of the workings and people on the other side of the lake saw timber hurled into the air. The mine caved in with a terrific rumble and air was shrieking out of the shaft for two days after." Since the new mill was on a hill away from the water, and since the shaft had long fallen into disuse, the flood failed to impede operations. Frobisher continued to harvest the tailings until 1954 when operations ceased forever.

Although Black Donald Mines truly became a ghost town, its story had not ended, for, in 1967, the waters invaded again, this time slowly, steadily and permanently. In an effort to harvest power from the rapids of the Madawaska River, the Ontario Hydro-Electric Power Commission was constructing a power dam at the site of the mining company's old power house. The waters of the new lake slowly crept over the site of the mine and mill, then stopped just short of the old townsite.

Black Donald Mines lies at the end of a twisting but scenic road west

These workers posed at a time when the Kingdon Mine led Canada in lead production.

Kingdon Mine lead smelter and tramway.

of Calabogie, an old lumber town. Although the houses no longer greet the visitor, their foundations abound in overgrown fields. Of the many buildings only the white frame Anglican church has survived, a silent sentinel over the blowing grasses and the lapping waters of the new lake. Recreational riches have replaced the mineral treasure as the area is now ideal for peaceful camping and tranquil canoeing.

KINGDON MINE

Some mining ghost towns have been the subject of magazine articles and newspaper columns, others of government reports. But Kingdon

Mine, which once enjoyed the reputation of being Canada's leading lead producer, lies among the grassy fields of an Ottawa River Island, forgotten and forlorn.

Several years passed between discovery and exploitation. In the 1860s, when the lead-bearing veins of Frontenac, Leeds, Bannockburn and other districts were arousing high hopes of a profitable lead industry, rumours of a large ore body on Morris Island, in the Ottawa River, began to spread. The deposit, however, lay untapped until 1884 when James Robertson drilled out several bags of galena and shipped them to Kingston. But Robertson lacked the funds to attempt large-scale operations and no further mining occurred until 1914 when the Kingdon Mining Smelting and Manufacturing Company leased the property from Robertson's estate. Because of the First World War lead was in great demand and the company launched an extensive mining and milling operation and, between 1914 and 1927, produced nearly all of Ontario's lead. By 1931 it had yielded more than 60 million pounds of lead valued in excess of $4 million, and 850,000 pounds of zinc.

Kingdon was famous not just for its production but also for the novel and safe methods of mining, milling and smelting. The Newman hearth furnace for refining lead from ore concentrates was safe, efficient, and non-polluting. "The process used at the Kingdon mine for the production of metallic lead...is novel in this Dominion. It was the writer's privilege to attempt to solve this problem, and the solution was found in the Newman improved hearth furnace... The old 'Scotch hearth' and its Americanized 'Moffet hearth' were limited in capacity, injurious to health and fatiguing to the hearth men... Mr. Newman's inventions and improvements...have removed all severe muscular labour...cut down losses in metal in fume and in slag and it is now possible to recover full 91% of the metal in the ore treated."

Kingdon Mine soon outgrew the established neighbouring towns. As the number of employees climbed to 160, and the future of the mine appeared promising, wives and children of the miners moved to the bustling new town. Its population soared to 250. The scene must have been impressive, with the boarding houses and cottages squeezed along two streets and dominated by the mill, smelter and tramways. While the community hall and company store were conveniently located in the centre of the village, the school was in a quieter locale to the north of the village. Unfortunately no church was nearer than that of the neighbouring town of Galetta. Here, too, company executives chose to live aloof from the miners. Using the island's deep soil to advantage, some miners operated small part-time farms which are evident to this day.

But, as shown throughout this chapter, no mine operates forever, and eastern Ontario's mineral deposits were seldom extensive. In 1931, following an influx of water from a hydro project on the Ottawa River, the mine closed. Most miners left immediately, some for nearby Arnprior or Ottawa, others for the mines of the north. Few remained.

A new road now links the island to the mainland to provide access to cottages in the swamp on the Ottawa River. Although the road crosses right through the old town, few motorists could appreciate its former fame for, of the town's 30 buildings, fewer than half a dozen still stand,

The village of Kingdon Mine as portrayed on a topographic map of 1930.

the remainder having been reduced to foundations overgrown by weeds, shrubs—even young trees—and the mill and smelter were dismantled years ago. Crushed limestone, from which the lead was extracted, covers several acres but, due to the dangerous condition of old shafts, these are sealed off by a sturdy chain link fence.

Of a town that was once prominent in the annals of mining in eastern Ontario, its vestiges lie forgotten in the woods and fields of this peaceful island in the Ottawa River.　　　　　　　　　　●

EPILOGUE

The words on the foregoing pages may be accurate today but only history tomorrow. For southern Ontario is an ever-changing area. Today's great land grab may, because of energy costs or land costs, suddenly die. Or it may accelerate, sparking still more ghost towns back to renewed life.

Even as I write these words scenes described on earlier pages are undergoing changes. Those which greet the ghost towner today may in several cases differ somewhat from when I visited the sites between 1974 and 1977. In at least one instance a ghost town—Keenansville— has lost two of its vacated landmarks. An abandoned house collapsed in flames as part of a practice exercise for local firemen. The old blacksmith shop too has since come tumbling down. Other towns are sprouting new buildings on old town lots long vacant and weedy.

But if the ghost towns described here may be changing, others await discovery. Since I began work on this book, many kind people have taken the trouble to write and advise me of other ghost towns. However, the lack of historical information about many of these places would have made a description of them only guess-work at best. Other parts of the province were just too far to get to. The far eastern part of Ontario near the Quebec border, and the extreme southwestern portion of Ontario may possess more ghost towns than I have discovered in my travels to date. Then there is northern Ontario.

The story of Northern Ontario differs markedly from that of southern Ontario. The harsh climate and rocky wilds discouraged the frontier fringe which engulfed southern Ontario from edging more than a few miles north of the French River or Lake Superior. Development here was based on resource exploitation or on transportation and has generally occurred only in the past one hundred years. Even to this day the population is sparsely distributed—the towns and cities far apart—separated by vast stretches of unsettled territory. Hidden in these remote reaches lie the uncountable, perhaps long forgotten, remains of lumber towns, mining towns and railway towns. Ancient Hudson Bay trading posts await the first view of the ghost towner. Someday I hope to direct my car and canoe to Ontario's northern reaches and open the pages on the untold tales of her decaying and forgotten ghost towns.

I hope too to fill in those gaps in the ever-changing story of southern Ontario's ghost towns, to peruse her eastern and western extremes and to follow through on some interesting leads which have come to light during the course of research for this book.

BIBLIOGRAPHY

Addison, Ottelyn, *Early Days in Algonquin Park*, McGraw-Hill Ryerson Ltd.

Anderson, C.E. & Co., *Province of Ontario Gazeteer and Directory*, 1869.

Armitage, Andrew, "Ghost Town was once Major Port", *Owen Sound Sun Times*, September 20, 1975.

Aylesworth, C.F., "The Hastings Roads", *Annual Report of the Association of Ontario Land Surveyors*, 1925.

Barker, James K., Huntsville, personal communication.

Barlow, Mrs. Ruth, Binbrook, Ontario, personal communication.

Barry, James, *Georgian Bay, The Sixth Great Lake*, Irwin & Co., Toronto, 1968.

Blackburn, Mrs. C.; Sandford, Mrs. S.; Moorecroft, Miss Alma; *Pilgrimage of Faith*, Madoc Review, 1974.

Bond, Courtney C.J., *The Ottawa Country*, Queen's Printer, Ottawa, 1968.

Bowell, MacKenzie, *Directory of the County of Hastings, 1860-61*, Belleville Intelligencer, 1860.

Boyce, Gerald E., Hastings County Historical Society, *Historic Hastings*, Hastings County Council, 1967.

Boyer, George W., *Early Days in Muskoka*, Herald-Gazette, Bracebridge, 1970.

The Bradstreet Company, *The Mercantile Agency Reference Book*, Toronto, 1913

Brunton, Sam, editor, *Notes and Sketches on the History of Parry Sound*, Parry Sound Historical Society, 1970.

Buchanan, Miss M., Toronto, personal communication.

Bull, Perkins Collection, Manuscript, Ontario Public Archives.

Calnan, A.L., "Allisonville, A Tale of a Country Village", *Picton Gazette Centennial Edition*, December 29, 1936.

Canada, Department of National Defence, *National Topographic Maps*, 1:50,000,
Rice Lake, 31D-1 East Half, 1928
Palmerston 40P-15, West Half, 1932.
"Arnprior, 31 F-8, West Half", 1926-9.

Cardwell Sentinel, Keenansville, 1878-82.

Carr, Mrs. Ross N., editor, *The Rolling Hills*, Manvers Township Council, 1967.

Carter, W.E.H., "Mines of Eastern Ontario", *Bureau of Mines Report*, Vol. L1, pt. 4, Ontario Department of Mines.

Centennial Review of the Township of Tossorontio, 1850-1950.

Charlton, R.R., *Duncrief 1835-1920.*

Cleverdon, Elsie, M., *An East Whitby Mosaic*, East Whitby Centennial Committee 1967.

Closky, Mr. Miles, Owen Sound, personal communication.

Davidson, T.A., *A New History of the County of Grey*, The Grey County Historical Society, 1972.

Dawson, G.M., *Summary Report on the Operations of the Geological Survey for the year 1899*, Geological Survey of Canada, Ottawa, 1900.

Dawson, Mary, "On an 1867 Assembly Line", *Yesterdays*, The Liberal, August 11, 1976, Richmond Hill, Ontario.

Dawson, Mary, "19th Century Vaughan Factory Recalled", *Yesterdays*, The Liberal, August 18, 1976, Richmond Hill, Ontario.

Demaine, Marjorie, editor, *Stories of Early Muskoka Days, Memoirs of W.H. Demaine*, Herald Gazette Press, Bracebridge, 1971.

Dominion Directory Co., *Lovells Province of Ontario Directory*, Montreal, 1871.

Drayton Enterprise, Drayton, Ontario 1874.

Dun and Bradstreet Company, *The Mercantile Agency Reference Book*, Toronto, 1933.

Dun and Bradstreet of Canada, *Reference Book*, Toronto, 1956.

Dun and Bradstreet of Canada, *Reference Book*, Toronto, 1975.

Elford, Jean T., *A History of Lambton County*, Sarnia, Ontario 1967.

Ennals, Peter, "Cobourg and Pt. Hope: The Struggle for the Control of the Back Country", *Perspectives on Landscape and Settlement in Nineteenth Century Ontario*, J. David Wood, editor, McClelland and Stewart, 1975.

Ermatinger, C.O., K.C., *The Talbot Regime*, The Municipal World Ltd., St. Thomas, 1904.

Essex County Sketches, Essex County Tourist Association, 1947.

First Report of the Bureau of Mines, 1891, Legislative Assembly of Ontario.

Folkes, P., *The History of the Bruce Peninsula, An Overview*, Ontario Ministry of Natural Resources, 1973.

Fox, W. Sherwood, *The Bruce Beckons*, University of Toronto Press.

Fraser, A., *A History of Ontario, Its Resources and Development*, 2 volumes, Toronto, 1907.

Fraser, L.R., *History of Muskoka*, Bracebridge, 1942.

Gazeteer and Directory of the County of Wellington, Irwin & Burnham, Toronto, 1867.

Gentilcore, R.L., and Wood, David, "A Military Colony in a Wilderness", *Perspectives on Landscape and Settlement in Nineteenth Century Ontario*, J. David Wood, editor, McClelland and Stewart, 1975.

Gibson, Thomas W., *Mining in Ontario*, Ontario Department of Mines, Kings Printer, Toronto, 1937.

Glazebrook, G.P. de T., *A History of Transportation in Canada*, Toronto, 1938.

A Glimpse of the Past, A Centennial History of Brantford and Brant County, Brant Historical Society, 1968.

Goodspeed, W.A. and C.L., *History of the County of Middlesex, Canada*, Toronto, 1889.

Guide Book and Atlas of Muskoka and Parry Sound Districts, H.R. Page & Co., Toronto, 1879.

Guillet, Edwin C., *Pioneer Days in Upper Canada*, University of Toronto Press, 1933.

Guillet, G.R., *Gypsum in Ontario*, Industrial Mineral Report #18, Ontario Department of Mines, 1964.

Hamilton, J.C., *The Georgian Bay*, J. Bain & Son, Toronto, 1893.

Hardman, John E., "The Kingdon Lead Mine", *Transactions of the Canadian Mining Institute*, Toronto, 1917.

Hess, A., "The Forgotten Names and Places", *Waterloo Historical Society #62*, 1974.

"Hikers Explore Village Ruins", *Kingston Whig-Standard*, October 5, 1975.

Historical Sketches of Markham Township 1793-1950. Historical Committee of municipal government.

"Historical Sketch of the Township of Belmont and Metheun", *Illustrated Historical Atlas of the County of Peterboro*.

History of Morris Township and Stories Relating to its Pioneer Days, 1856-1956, Morris Historical Committee, 1956.

A History of Peel County, Corporation of the County of Peel, 1967.

Hunter, A.F., *A History of Simcoe County*, 2 vol., Barrie, 1909.

Illustrated Atlas of Lanark County; Illustrated Atlas of Renfrew County, H. Beldon & Co., Toronto, 1881.

Illustrated Historical Atlas of the County of Carleton, H. Beldon & Co., Toronto 1879.

Illustrrated Historical Atlas of the County of Elgin, H.R. Page & Co., Toronto, 1877.

Illustrated Historical Atlas of the Counties of Frontenac and Lennox and Addington, H. Beldon & Co., Toronto, 1878.

Illustrated Historical Atlas of the County of Grey, H. Beldon & Co., Toronto, 1880.

Illustrated Historical Atlas of the County of Haldimand, H.R. Page & Co., Toronto 1879.

Illustrated Historical Atlas of the Counties of Hastings and Prince Edward, H. Beldon & Co., Toronto, 1878.

Illustrated Historical Atlas of the County of Huron, H. Beldon & Co., Toronto, 1879.

Illustrated Historical Atlas of the Counties of Leeds and Grenville, Mika Publishing Co., Belleville, 1973. (Reproduction).

Illustrated Historical Atlas of the County of Middlesex, H.R. Page & Co., Toronto, 1878.

Illustrated Historical Atlas of the Counties of Northumberland and Durham, H. Beldon & Co., Toronto, Mika Silk Screening (reproduction), 1972.

Illustrated Historical Atlas of the County of Peel, Walker & Mills Co., Toronto, 1877.

Illustrated Atlas of the County of Simcoe, H. Beldon & Co., Toronto, 1881.

Illustrated Historical Atlas of the County of Wellington, Historical Atlas Publishing Co., Toronto, 1906.

Illustrated Historical Atlas of the County of York, Miles & Co., Toronto, 1878.

Johnston, Wm., *History of the County of Perth*, Stratford, 1903.

Jones, R.L., *History of Agriculture in Ontario, 1613-1880*, University of Toronto Press, 1946.

Jury, Wilfrid and McLeod, Elsie, *The Nine-Mile Portage from Kempenfeldt Bay to the Nottawasaga River*, Museum Bulletin #11, Museum of Indian archaeology, University of Western Ontario, London, Ontario, 1956.

Kennedy, Clyde C., *The Upper Ottawa Valley*, Renfrew County Council, Pembroke, Ontario, 1970.

Kirkconnell, Watson, and F.L. MacArthur, *County of Victoria Centennial History*, Victoria County Council, Lindsay, 1947.

Laidler, George, "The Nottawasaga Portage, Simcoe County, Ontario", *Ontario Historical Society Papers and Records*, Vol. 35, Toronto, 1943.

Lawiston, Victor, *Lambton's Hundred Years, 1849-1949.*

Legget, Robert, *The Rideau Waterway,* University of Toronto Press, 1955.

Leitch, Adelaide, *The Visible Past, the Pictorial History of Simcoe County,* Ryerson Press, Toronto, 1967.

Lincoln County, 1856-1956, Lincoln County Council, St. Catharines, Ontario 1956.

Lockwood, Glenn J., *Kitley 1795-1975,* Prescott, 1975.

Lovell's Gazeteer and Directory of the Province of Ontario, Montreal 1882.

The Lovely Townships of Grey and Bruce, Talks Delivered on Radio Station CFOS by Kris Morris, published by the Victoria and Grey Trust Company.

Lower, A.R.M. and Innis, H.A., *Settlement of the Forest and Mining Frontier,* Toronto, 1936.

Mackay, R.W.S., *The Canada Directory,* Montreal, 1851.

MacCrimmon, Mr. Graydon, Kaladar, personal communication.

Mack, H., *Historical Highlights of Wellington County,* 1956.

Marshall, John U., *Central Places in the Queens Bush,* unpublished M.A. Thesis, University of Minnesota, Minneapolis, Minnesota, 1964.

Marsh, E.L., *A History of the County of Grey,* Grey County Council, 1931.

McClenton, William, Black Bank, Ontario, personal communication.

McFie, Mr. J., Parry Sound, personal communication.

McGill, Jean S., *A Pioneer History of the County of Lanark,* Toronto, 1968.

McIvor, Marilyn P., *Turkey Point Provincial Park, Fort Norfolk, Charlotteville and the War of 1812,* Ontario Ministry of Culture and Recreation, 1975.

McKay, Wm. A., *The Pickering Story,* Township of Pickering Historical Society.

McKean, F.K., *Railroad Reaches Town; A History of Railroading in Parry Sound and Georgian Bay,* Parry Sound Historical Society, 1962.

McKean, F.K., "Depot Harbour, The First Seaway Terminal", *Inland Seas,* Vol. 21 #3, 1965.

McKean, J., *Depot Harbour, "A Profile of a Railroad Town",* unpublished essay, 1968.

McKenzie, Ruth, *Leeds and Grenville, Their First 200 Years,* McClelland and Stewart, 1967.

McKessock, Mrs. Mary, Chatsworth, Ontario, personal communication.

Meen, V.B., *Geology of the Grimsthorpe-Barrie Area,* Ontario Department of Mines, Annual Report #51, pt. IV, 1942.

Mights Directory, Dominion of Canada Gazeteer and Classified Business Directory 1899.

Mika, Nick and Helma, editors, *Community Spotlight, Leeds, Frontenac, Lennox and Addington, Prince Edward Counties,* Mika Publishing Co., Belleville, 1974.

Mike, Nick and Helma, ed., *Community Spotlight,* Belleville, 1974.

Miller, Marilyn G., *Small Scale Mining in the South Shield Region of Eastern Ontario,* Ontario Ministry of Natural Resources, 1976.

"Mines of Ontario", *Ontario Bureau of Mines, Seventeenth Annual Report,* Kings Printer, 1908.

Mitchell and Co., *County of Carlton and City of Ottawa, Directory for 1864-5.*

Morenz, Mrs. H., Dashwood, Ontario, personal communication.

Moyer, Bill, *Bill Moyer's Waterloo County Diary,* CHYM Kitchener, Ontario.

Mulcahy and Cashman, *Directory of Simcoe County 1866-7.*

Mulmur, The Story of a Township, Mulmur Historical Committee, 1951.

Murray, F.B., *Muskoka and Haliburton 1615-1875,* Champlain Society, Toronto, 1963.

Newton, Mrs. Derek, London, Ontario, personal communication.

Ontario Gazeteer and Directory 1884-5, R.L. Polk and Company, Toronto, 1885.

Ontario Publishing Co., *Gazeteer and Directory of Ontario, 1901-2, 1907-8,* Ingersoll, Ontario.

Parry Sound Colonial, Parry Sound, Ontario, 1892.

Patterson, G.C., "Land Settlement in Upper Canada 1783-1840, *16th Report of the Department of Archives for the Province of Ontario, 1920,* Toronto, 1921.

Peebles, J. Elaine, *The Nine-Mile Portage and Willow Creek Depot 1814-1835,* Ontario Ministry of Natural Resources, 1974.

Picton's 100 Years, Prince Edward County Old Boys Reunion, Official Souvenir Book, 1937.

Porter, C., *An Inventory of the Historical Resources of Wasaga Beach,* Ontario Ministry of Natural Resources, 1973.

Putnam, D.F., editor, *Canadian Regions, A Georgraphy of Canada,* J.M. Dent and Sons, 1952.

Putnam, D.F., and L.J. Chapman, *The Physiography of Southern Ontario,* University of Toronto Press 1951.

Reeve, H., *The History of the Township of Hope,* 1967.

Renfrew Mercury, Renfrew, Ontario, 1885-95.

Rennie, Jas. A., *Louth Township, Its People and Its Past,* Louth Township Citizens Centennial

Committee, 1966.

Reynolds, Nila, *In Quest of Yesterday*, Provisional County of Haliburton.

Richardson, A.H., *R.D.H.P. Valley Conservation Report*, Ontario Department of Planning and Development, 1956. (Rouge, Duffin, Highland and Petticoat Rivers).

Robertson, Norman, *The History of the County of Bruce*, Bruce County Historical Society, 1906.

Robinson, C. Blackett, *History of the County of Peterboro*, 1884.

"Romance of Forgotten Towns", *Western Ontario Historical Notes*, Vol. XXI, #2, Sept., 1965.

Rose, E.R., Iron Deposits of Eastern Ontario and Adjoining Quebec, *Geological Survey of Canada, Bulletin 45*, Ottawa, 1958.

Saunders, A., *The Algonquin Story*, Ontario Department of Lands and Forests, Toronto, 1947.

Scadding, H., *Toronto of Old*, Toronto, 1873.

Schmid, Mrs. Helen, Hope Township, personal communication.

Scott, James, *The Settlement of Huron County*, Ryerson Press, 1966.

Shelburne Economist, Shelburne, Ontario, 1884-1894.

Smith, Wm. H., *Smiths Canadian Gazeteer 1846*, Coles Canadiana Collection

Smith, W.W., *Gazeteer and Directory of the County of Grey, 1865-6*, Toronto, 1865.

Spelt, J., *Urban Development in South-Central Ontario*, McClelland and Stewart, Toronto, 1972.

Spragge, G.W., "Colonization Roads in Canada West", *Ontario History*, Vol. XLIX, #57.

Stevens, E., *Colonization Road Survey*, Ontario Ministry of Natural Resources.

Strathroy Ace, Strathroy, Ontario 1871.

Taylor, A.W., *Our Todays and Yesterdays, A History of the Township of North Dumfries and the Village of Ayr*, North Dumfries and Ayr Centennial Committee, 1967.

Tough, George W., *Rise and Decline — Hamlets and their Hinterlands in a Small Shield Area*, unpublished B.A. thesis, University of Western Ontario, London, Ontario, 1964.

Tomlinson, Mr. William, Tweed, Ontario, personal communication.

The Township of Seneca History, Seneca Centennial Historical Committee, 1967.

Tremaine's Atlas of the County of Middlesex, 1862.

Tremaine's Atlas of the Counties of Lincoln and Welland, 1862.

Tweedsmuir History of Mt. Healey, Mt. Healey Women's Institute, Mt. Healey, Ont.

Union Publishing Co., *Farmers and Business Directory for the Counties of Bruce, Grey, Middlesex, Oxford, Simcoe*, Vol. IX, Ingersoll, Ontario 1896.

Wagar, Mrs. L., Simcoe County Archives, Midhurst, Ontario, personal communication.

Walling, H.F., *Illustrated Historical Atlas of the County of Carleton*, 1863.

Walling, H.F., *Illustrated Historical Atlas of the Counties of Leeds and Grenville*, Kingston, 1861.

White, Alex, Robertsville, personal communication.

Whiting, Brenda-Lee, "The Craigmont Corundum Boom, 1900-1913", *Canadian Geographical Journal*, Vol. 90, #4, April 1975.

William, Bradley, Ballycroy, personal communication.

Wilson, M.E., *Arnprior-Quyon and Maniwaki Areas Ontario and Quebec*, Geological Survey of Canada, Memoir 136, Ottawa, 1924.

18th Annual Report of the Waterloo Historical Society, 1930.

PHOTO CREDITS

Public Archives of Canada: 8, 24, 31, 37(L), 52, 141, 143, 151(B), 154(T), 156, 165, 172, 174, 186, 187, 190(T).

Ron Brown: 20, 21, 24(B), 26, 27(B), 29, 37(R), 47, 49, 50, 55, 59, 61(L), 65, 73, 76, 81, 86, 90, 93, 94, 103, 106, 110(C), 113, 118, 128, 131, 135, 139(B), 146, 147, 164, 178, 185(B).

Ontario Public Archives: 23, 58(B), 63, 133, 139, 160, 166(B), 167(T), 177.

N.A. Patterson: 27(T).

Hastings County Museum: 43.

Maxwell McLean: 89.

Canadian Baptist Archives: 110(T & B).

United Church of Canada Archives: 125.

Miss A. Moorecroft: 127.

G. Moroz: 139(T).

Prof. H.U. Rose: 140.

Mrs. Mary Pigeon: 144.

Ontario Ministry of Natural Resources: 144-145, 160.

Toronto Public Library: 151(T).

S. Fox: 154(B).

Ray Tanner: 166(T), 167(B).

Ontario Bureau of Mines Reports: 171, 185(T).

Geological Survey of Canada: 176(T), 180(B), 182, 184, 190(B).

Ontario Hydro: 188.

INDEX